How To Help Your Teenager Grow Up

By Leland E. Glover, Ph.D.

www.sunvillagepublications.com

How To Help Your Teenager Grow Up
By Leland E. Glover, Ph.D.

Copyright © 2010

www.sunvillagepublications.com

Cover design by www.WebCopyAlchemy.com

Checklist for Parents

Do you—

- ☐ Recognize the emotional and physical problems your child faces in growing up?
- ☐ Understand normal adolescent growth and development and how your teen-ager follows the pattern?
- ☐ Encourage your youngster to establish wholesome friendships?
- ☐ Guide your child in becoming socially competent?
- ☐ Appreciate how your teen-ager feels about himself?
- ☐ Help your youngster to get the most out of junior high school and high school? To prepare for college?

Dr. Glover reminds us:

"Teen-agers need parents today more than they have ever needed them before. They need parents who encourage them to face life's problems realistically, courageously, persistently, not as children or as adults, but as adolescents."

To

this nation's parents, teachers, and
community leaders who work with
children and youth to build a better
tomorrow.

Foreword

Adolescence, the transition period between childhood and adulthood, is an exciting, challenging time for teen-agers and parents alike. It is a time for discarding childish habits, for abandoning immature ways of behaving in favor of mature ones. It is a period of personal confusion, self-discovery, continual readjustment. It is a dramatic stage of development in which youngsters definitely need parents, but in ways that are different from their childhood needs.

Parents everywhere want their teen-agers to grow up to be reliable, responsible citizens, successful marriage partners, and competent, conscientious fathers and mothers. To help youngsters do this, parents must understand them, accept them, recognize their normal needs and desires; furthermore, they must help them find acceptable, constructive ways of satisfying those needs and desires.

Dr. Glover's book provides much useful information, many fresh ideas and sound suggestions for guiding teenagers in the right direction. I think it will prove to be a useful guide not only for parents but also for teachers, ministers, physicians, psychologists, social workers, recreation leaders, and other adults who work with teen-age boys and girls.

NADINA R. KAVINOKY, M.D.

Preface

This book is directed to adults whose children are or will soon be adolescents. Its purpose is to help them guide their youngsters through pubescence to young adulthood —a span of years that varies considerably among individuals, extending generally from the eleventh, twelfth, or thirteenth year to the nineteenth or twentieth year, and from the sixth or seventh grade in school to approximately the first year beyond high school.

Serious consideration of adolescent development leads naturally to identifying the problems teen-agers face: how to understand themselves, make friends, become socially competent; how to resolve important questions regarding sex, work, money, and cars; how to regard school, the church, the adult community; how to plan educationally and vocationally for future success; how to prepare intelligently for the responsibilities of impending adulthood. Careful analyses are made of these problems, and possible methods of coping with them are offered the reader.

Parents and other adults who work with teen-agers as well as teachers of college-level classes in marriage education and family living, secondary education, and adolescent psychology, may find this book helpful. High school counselors may want to make it available to parents of student-counselees.

Parents who participate in child-study groups, such as those conducted by the Parent-Teachers Association, will be especially interested in the books, films, and pamphlet sources listed at the end of the book.

Grateful acknowledgement is made to the many individuals who made valuable suggestions and to the following organizations and institutions, which contributed information to help make this book possible: Allstate Insurance Company; the American Association of School

Administrators; the American Council on Education; the American Dental Association; the American Driver Education Association; the American Institute of Family Relations; the American Medical Association; the American Personnel and Guidance Association; the American School Counselor Association; the Association of Casualty and Surety Companies; the Billig Clinic; the Bobbs-Merrill Company, Inc.; the California Congress of Parents and Teachers; the California Medical Association; the California State Department of Education; the California State Department of Motor Vehicles; the California State Highway Patrol; the California Teachers Association; the Child Study Association of America; the College Entrance Examination Board; Columbia University; Educational Testing Service; the El Monte (California) Union High School District; the Florence Crittenton Home; the Ford Foundation; General Motors Corporation; the Gesell Institute of Child Development; the Institute for Living; the John Hancock Mutual Life Insurance Company; the Los Angeles Unified School District; the Metropolitan Life Insurance Company; the National Congress of Parents and Teachers; the National Council of Family Relations; the National Education Association; the National Institute for Mental Health; the National Safety Council; the National Vocational Guidance Association; the Los Angeles County Superintendent of Schools Office; The Los Angeles Police Department; the Parents' Institute; the Pasadena Child Guidance Clinic; Purdue University; the San Marino (California) Unified School District; the Santa Barbara County Schools; *Scholastic Magazine;* Selective Service; *Sexology Magazine;* the United States Department of Health, Education, and Welfare; the United States Department of Labor; the United States Public Health Service; the University of Illinois; the University of Iowa; the University of Maryland; the University of Michigan; the University of Nebraska; and the University of Southern California.

LELAND E. GLOVER

Contents

Chapter 1

Identifying Teen-agers' Problems

"OUR EARTH IS degenerate these latter days; there are signs that the world is speedily coming to an end; bribery and corruption are common; children no longer obey their parents; and the end of the world is evidently approaching." This message was carved on an Assyrian stone tablet that dates from about 2800 B.C.

Twenty-four centuries later—about 400 B.C.—the great Greek philosopher Socrates expressed his opinion of the younger generation in these words: "Children now love luxury; they show disrespect for elders and love chatter in place of exercise. Children are now tyrants, not the servants of their households. They no longer rise when elders enter the room. They contradict their parents, chatter before company, gobble up dainties at the table, cross their legs, and tyrannize over their teachers."

Human beings have not changed much in the past few thousand years, but civilization has. If Socrates and the disillusioned Assyrian who carved the tablet were to re-appear and live with us today, they would be confused, to say the least: radio, television, jet planes, sonic booms, electronic computers, Christmas, guided missiles, the stock market, the Fourth of July, the Mafia, sports cars, congressional investigations, Madison Avenue, hydrogen bombs, the fifth amendment, working mothers, polio shots, drive-in movies, freeways, hot dogs, hamburgers, chocolate malts, french fries, filter cigarettes, space travel. But there is one thing those two distinguished gentlemen would not be confused about in the slightest: The younger generation is still going to the dogs—just as it has been doing for the past five thousand years!

Today's teachers, over whom youngsters "tyrannize" as before, are a bit more optimistic about the younger generation than was Socrates. They say, "Let's be fair—youth is not perfect and never has been; but there is evidence to support the belief that the younger generation of today is generally serious, capable, and courageous in spite of rather discouraging world conditions. Today's youth is our only hope for tomorrow."[1]

Today's parents, whose children "no longer obey," are more optimistic than the ancient Assyrian. They know that youngsters need room in which to grow and develop mentally, emotionally, and spiritually, and that they need guidance by parents to help them grow in the right directions. Parents search continually, therefore, for better ways of working with children to produce the desired results.

The problems today's teen-agers face are very difficult to solve because they require many adjustments and compromises that are often opposed to nature. Teen-agers want, for example, to become independent and self-sufficient; yet they are necessarily encouraged to prolong their dependency, stay in school, refrain from working full time, postpone marriage and parenthood, accept and abide by the laws that classify them as children.

Most teen-agers are sexually mature and biologically capable of becoming parents. They must control their sexual urges, however, because they are not yet prepared emotionally, financially, or occupationally to meet the responsibilities of parenthood. This dilemma is intensified by the heavy emphasis on physical attractiveness in our culture. Boys and girls are encouraged to make themselves attractive to members of the opposite sex and to mix freely heterosexually in varying states of dress and undress at dances, parties, swimming pools, the beach, and in other settings that are sexually stimulating.

The value assigned money and material goods in our culture adds to the teen-ager's inner conflicts. He grows up

---

[1] Statement of belief issued by classroom teachers through the California Teachers Association.

in an economically competitive society; yet he must suppress the urge to drop out of school and get a job to satisfy his desire for money. He is encouraged instead to get an education that may require several years beyond high school but will eventually put him in a more favorable position to compete successfully.

The automobile, America's most popular status symbol, causes many problems for teen-agers and parents. Most teen-agers are physically and intellectually mature enough to operate a car and take care of it; yet they are seldom financially able to keep one, nor are they always emotionally mature enough to drive. Furthermore, they are not legally permitted to drive until they have attained the minimum age specified by the state.

School brings problems as well as joys. America's teenagers participate in the most comprehensive and complex system of free public education in the world; yet universal, compulsory, mass education is often confusing to the individual. Some youngsters think the work is too difficult; they get discouraged, want to quit. Others find school too easy and become bored; they need to be challenged with work that is more difficult. According to surveys, however, most students are satisfied; they say school meets their needs; they seek no changes. Yet teen-agers believe generally that school is not "fife" but merely a substitute for it that may prepare them for "the real thing."

Morality causes teen-agers much concern. They are often confused about what constitutes "right" and "wrong" in human behavior. Their attitudes perhaps reflect the confusion of values of adults in modern civilization.

Religion occupies adolescents' minds and emotions more frequently than many of us realize. Teen-agers need religion and seek it. Yet most of them question their own beliefs and then feel guilty for having questioned them. This behavior pattern is normal in our culture; it reflects the complexity of a free society. There are many religions in America, and often several sects of each religion. Millions of citizens have no serious religious convictions at all. Teen-agers question their own beliefs because they are adolescents and because so many people who are as intelligent as they are hold quite different beliefs.

The world of work holds many threats and some unanswerable questions for most teen-agers. There are thousands of different kinds of jobs in our complex world. Teen-agers searching for the "right" occupation seem sometimes like mice in a laboratory maze trying to find the single path to the goal that spells success.

Marriage holds many mysteries for adolescents. They think ordinarily that marriage is a state of eternal bliss, punctuated periodically perhaps by the arrival of a baby. Yet they are told continually that marriage is risky and serious, that every third or fourth marriage in America ends in divorce. They see the seamy side of marriage dramatized often on television and in the movies: infidelity, adultery, divorce, courtroom battles over custody of children, husbands and wives arguing continually, fighting, threatening to kill one another—and sometimes doing it. These behaviors are not unreal, of course, and they are unfortunate. Some youngsters do not have to watch TV or go to the movies to witness such unwholesome marital relationships. They know from personal observation in the neighborhood—perhaps in their own homes—that many marriages that endure are not really happy or successful.

Finally, world conditions and international tensions cause teen-agers much concern—and well they should. Will there be another world war? If it comes, can anyone survive? If someone survives, what will there be left to live for? Teen-agers, according to recent surveys, tend generally to reply to such questions with an answer such as this: "What's the use of trying to live a good, clean, moral life today when you're likely to be vaporized by a hydrogen bomb tomorrow?" This attitude of hopelessness is sometimes reflected in delinquent-like behavior by normal teen-agers.

Parents admit that they are often as confused as teen-agers about some of these problems. They have lived through them and gained many insights; yet they have failed to solve the problems. They know by experience that some problems cannot be solved to one's complete satisfaction, while others seem to solve themselves in due time. They know also that some problems must be endured. This is a lesson most teen-agers have not yet learned.

Teen-agers are generally not happy about the world conditions they are inheriting—an idealistic attitude that reflects the nature of adolescence as much as the world conditions themselves. Adolescents do not often forgive adults their shortcomings, which are admittedly many. The fact that grown-ups have failed to solve all of life's problems proves conclusively to the adolescent that they are hopeless incompetents, and bunglers!

Some parents, feeling that a good offense is the best defense against adolescent aggression, do battle with teenagers who display normal hostility against grown-ups. This approach to the "problem" is wrong, of course, and leads inevitably to increased hostility, tension, and greater psychological distance between parents and adolescent.

How parents can help their teen-agers

What can you do to help your teen-ager live successfully through this difficult period? Many suggestions will be found in the pages that follow. Here are four brief recommendations that are generally useful:

Be patient. Try to understand and accept the fact that your teen-ager is experiencing a stage of growth and development that makes him see himself, you, and the world as quite different from what he has known before. Realize that he is up against some serious problems that are not necessarily of his own making but are inherent in adolescence or in our complex civilization. Remember too that as a child he thought you knew everything; now he realizes that you are not omniscient.

Listen, listen, listen. Listen to your teen-ager, even though you do not necessarily understand him or agree with what he says. Hear him out Do not try to force your own ideas and convictions onto him, even when you think absolutely that you are right and he is wrong. He is probably trying to find his way through the woods of adolescence and wants to verbalize his confusion. This he must do if he is to find his own way to maturity.

Trust your teen-ager. Encourage your youngster to decide most things for himself, to be self-sufficient within the limits of his maturity. Do not make up his mind for him as if he were an incompetent child. Do not expect him, on the other hand, to behave always like an adult when he is still an adolescent.

Keep your sense of humor. Many things that normal teen-agers do seem unnecessary at times and annoying to adults, many of whom have forgotten how it feels to be an adolescent. Adults should try to understand why adolescents act as they do and not become upset when their youngsters behave as normal, healthy teen-agers are supposed to behave.

SUMMARY

This chapter identified some of the problems America's teen-agers face and suggested ways parents can help their youngsters meet them.

The next chapter will discuss growth and development during adolescence and suggest ways parents can help teen-agers cope with their "new" bodies.

Chapter 2

Adolescent Growth and Development

"OUR SON BILL is growing like a weed," says Mrs. Jones, a typical mother. "He's only thirteen years old, but already he's as tall as his father. And he's still growing up—not out, just up. Honestly, it looks as if he'll never stop growing!"

Rapid growth during preadolescence has special meanings. The growth spurt that Bill Jones is experiencing signals his impending sexual maturity. This pattern of sudden growth prior to puberty (sexual maturity) conforms to nature's blueprint. It is caused by a hormone from the pituitary, a tiny endocrine gland located in a recess on the underside of the brain.

When Bill reaches the peak of the growth spurt, another pituitary hormone will stimulate his gonads (sex glands), making them mature rapidly and produce spermatozoa (sex cells). When that happens, Bill will have attained sexual maturity. He will have crossed the invisible line that separates childhood from adolescence.

Boys and girls mature at different rates. Girls experience the same growth phenomenon that Bill Jones is experiencing, but they mature a year or two earlier than boys. They start growing rapidly as a rule when they are nine, ten, or eleven years old, reach the peak of the growth spurt when they are eleven, twelve, or thirteen years old, and then become sexually mature. Boys, on the other hand, start growing rapidly when they are eleven, twelve, or thirteen years old, reach the peak of the growth spurt when they are thirteen, fourteen, or fifteen years old, and then become sexually mature.

Physical symptoms of sexual maturity include menstruation and seminal emissions. Sexual maturity is marked by

19

the onset of menstruation (menarche) in girls and by the presence of semen in boys. Most girls tell their mother when the menses appear. Boys are almost invariably secretive about seminal emissions because they suspect that having them is "wrong."

Boys discharge semen ordinarily either in response to a sex dream while they are asleep (nocturnal emission, or "wet dream") or as a climax of self-stimulation (masturbation) when they are awake. They feel guilty about it in either case, and that is probably the reason they do not' ordinarily discuss it with their parents.

Adolescent growth patterns tend to confuse boy-girl social relationships. The marked difference between the maturation time-tables of the two sexes creates problems. It causes most seventh-grade girls, for example, to be heavier and taller than most seventh-grade boys. The difference between the sexes is social as well as physical. Twelve-year-old boys, for example, are still interested in such activities as pulling girls' ponytails, kicking their, shins, and playing baseball with other boys. Twelve-year-old girls, on the other hand, are likely to be interested in boys, love, romance, and adventure.

Young adolescent girls, being larger and emotionally more mature than boys their age, usually choose older boys as companions because they are their equals from the point of view of maturity. This pattern of younger girls getting together with older boys is as ancient as the human race. It prevails generally through adolescence into adulthood and marriage. That is the reason why husbands are usually two or three years older than their wives. (The average age in America in 1959 for first marriage was 19.9 years for brides and 22.5 years for grooms—an age difference of almost three years.)

Abnormal rates of maturing may signal trouble. The normal age range for reaching puberty is fairly well established; however, the age at which a specific boy or girl will become sexually mature cannot be predicted accurately. The youngster's own built-in development timetable will decide this matter.

Parents should not fret if their child's growth pattern is within the normal range. If it is clearly outside this range, however, they should seek medical advice, for strange things can happen when youngsters with severely distorted growth patterns are not treated. A little girl in Chile, for example, became a mother when she was only five years old. This fact seems even more remarkable when one recalls that the child was sexually mature and fertile when she conceived nine months earlier. Gynecologists discover occasionally, at the other extreme, an otherwise normal woman in her twenties who is not yet sexually mature and who is not able, therefore, to conceive. Medical treatment can usually slow down the maturation rate if it is too fast or speed it up if it is too slow.

Secondary growth characteristics indicate sexual maturity. Boys and girls who have recently reached puberty develop new physical characteristics. Most important, they stop growing upward and start filling out. Girls' breasts become steadily larger, and their hips get wider. Their shoulders look deceptively narrower than before because of this contrast, and their waists look thinner. Fatty tissue forms gradually about the hips and thighs, and the muscles become softer and more pliable.

Boys' shoulders become broader but their waists remain small: their torsos take on the shape of a modified "V." Their muscles tend to grow strong and firm. There are, of course, many individual differences in teen-agers' figures and body-builds and in the rates at which they develop.

Puberty is reflected also by the appearance in both sexes of short, coarse, "grown-up" hair in the pubic region, under the arms, and on the legs. It shows up also on some boys' chests, shoulders, and forearms. The fuzz or down on boys' faces darkens gradually and gives way to whiskers. Most boys have to start shaving soon after puberty.

Adolescence demands additional attention to cleanliness and personal hygiene. Teen-agers regard shaving as evidence that a boy is almost grown up. Yet removing facial hair is only one of many personal factors that require considerable attention during adolescence. Most mature girls shave the hair from their legs because they consider it unsightly. They shave under their arms also for the same reason, and because absence of hair makes deodorants much more effective. Many boys too remove the hair from under their arms and apply deodorants. This practice is no longer thought to be the mark of a sissy; big, strong, masculine fellows do it too—in spite of warnings to the contrary by distributors of so-called "men's deodorants."

Skin conditions and body odors change when youngsters become sexually mature. The teen-ager's oil ducts (sebaceous glands) work overtime. They get clogged up some times, causing blackheads, pimples, and other unsightly blemishes. Acne, the term used to describe such conditions, has been appropriately called "the scourge of youth." Some young people seem predisposed to acne while others are not bothered with it at all.

Doctors report that some acne-ridden teen-agers respond fairly well to diet therapy, which consists mainly of avoiding sweets and fatty foods. Washing the face frequently and thoroughly with a soap of good quality and warm water is a *must*. Some physicians recommend the use of a small mechanical instrument that helps remove the core of pimples and blackheads, thus relieving the blocked oil ducts. If your youngster has such a problem, ask your family physician's opinion on this gadget, and secure one if he thinks it would help. Incidentally, medical research in chemistry for relief from acne appears promising.

Sweat glands in adolescents work overtime too, and their products are noticeably different from the perspiration of young children. Bacteria thrive on oil-laden, post-pubescent skin products, especially under the arms and in the anal, genital, and mammary regions of the body. This means that skin and hair that are neglected soon develop offensive odors; consequently, teen-agers must bathe and shampoo regularly and wear clean, fresh clothing if they are to avoid being offensive to other people.

Dental care during adolescence is imperative. According to the American Dental Association, teeth tend to decay more rapidly during adolescence than before. Teen-agers should develop a routine of dental care and stick to it. An adequate program would include regular visits to the dentist every six months and brushing the teeth thoroughly at least twice each day (after breakfast, for example, and before going to bed) and a third time, if possible, after lunch.

Adolescents need a minimum schedule for adequate self-maintenance. Teen-agers should impose upon themselves a schedule for care of their persons. Minimum requirements should include the following:

A daily bath with plenty of warm water and good quality toilet soap.

Shampoos as frequently as necessary to keep the hair and scalp fresh and clean. (The old idea that washing hair frequently may damage it is a myth.)

Removal of underarm hair when necessary, and daily use of an effective deodorant.

Use of other cosmetic preparations with pleasing scents, such as talcum powder, foot powder, and after-shave lotion for boys; body powder, perfume, and toilet water for girls. These items should be used in good taste as the occasion demands.

Shaving by boys when necessary.

Brushing teeth regularly two or three times each day.

A daily change to fresh undergarments, stockings or socks, and other clothing that comes in direct contact with the skin.

Making sure that outer clothing is fresh, neat, and well cared for. Of course, you may add requirements to this list.

Parents may help youngsters establish good habits of personal care. Teen-agers should ordinarily work out their own schedules of self-maintenance rather than have them imposed by adults. However, parents can help them get started. The first step is, of course, to grant boys and girls rights to the facilities they need (bathroom, laundry room, and so on). The second step is to give them the necessary equipment and supplies. Here is a partial list of the items teen-agers need that parents should supply:

Soap, shampoo, wash cloths, towels.

Safety razor or electric shaver and related equipment.

Deodorants and other cosmetic preparations appropriate to the sexes and to the individuals. Combs, brushes, mirrors, and other paraphernalia that encourage youngsters to look at themselves and make themselves look good.

Toothbrushes and toothpaste or toothpowder. Clothes brushes, hangers, clothes closet, etc., to keep coats, suits, trousers, skirts, and dresses looking neat. Shoe maintenance equipment: polishes; cleaning and polishing cloths and brushes.

You will probably find yourself adding other items to this list.

Menstruation poses special problems for girls. Adolescent girls must grow accustomed to menstruation, a normal function of the body that they commonly call periods or monthlies.

Mothers, physicians, and school personnel (home-making teachers, school nurses) should prepare young girls to deal with menstruation before they experience the first menstrual period. Girls should know ahead of time what menstruation is, how it works, and why it happens as it does. All girls should be given sanitary napkins and tampons and taught how to use them.

Some teen-age girls need medical help with problems that grow out of menstruation. For example, they may suffer premenstrual backaches and the blues. They may need mild medication to relieve menstrual cramps. Many girls find relief through the use of regular exercises that stretch certain ligaments of the legs, pelvis, and lower back. An exercise routine devised by Harvey Billig, M.D., is used in many public schools' physical education classes for girls. The instructions for this routine, known as *The Billig Stretch,* appear below. They should be followed carefully. The exercise is best done under the guidance of a physical therapist if one is available.

Stand alongside a wall with your *left* side next to the wall. Keep your feet together, about eighteen inches from the wall. Keep your legs straight and your knees locked so that you won't bend your legs. Keep your hips *tucked under.*

Place your *left* arm against the wall, shoulder height. Be sure that the palm of your hand, your forearm, and your elbow all are in contact with the wall.

Place your right hand against the hollow of your right hip joint. Then, slowly and deliberately, push your hips forward and toward the wall as far as they will go.

Slowly return to starting position.

Now turn around and stand alongside the wall with your *right* side next to the wall. Keep your feet together, about eighteen inches from the wall. Keep your legs straight and your knees locked so you won't bend your legs. Keep your hips *tucked under.*

Place your *right* arm against the wall, shoulder height. Be sure that the palm of your hand, your forearm, and your elbow all are in contact with the wall.

Place your left hand against the hollow of your left hip joint. Then, slowly and deliberately, push your hips forward and toward the wall as far as they will go.

Slowly return to starting position.

Dr. Billig suggests three exercise sessions each day, preferably one in the morning, one at noon, and one at night. He advises girls to go through the entire routine three times each session.

Girls who are seriously troubled with menstrual cramps and feelings of depression should see their family physician. He may treat them himself, or he may send them to a gynecologist. If medical efforts fail to modify or relieve the symptoms, it may be wise to try psychological or psychiatric help. Otherwise, the youngster must learn to live with the problem.

Few girls suffer prolonged discomfort during their periods. Menstruation is a normal function of the female body. It is not an illness and should not be treated as one. Most girls do the same things during menstruation that they do at other times—dance, swim, play tennis, ride horseback. It is wrong to pamper girls who experience normal menstrual discomfort and encourage them to make a big thing of it. Most teen-age girls will be menstruating for the next twenty-five or thirty-five years; it is to their advantage, therefore, to adjust themselves satisfactorily to the process while they are young.

Boys, too, have special problems. Adolescent boys have problems that are unique to their sex. The changing voice is an example. Girls' voices become richer in quality, but boys' voices change both in quality and in pitch. The male voice drops an octave (eight full notes). In some boys this transition is anything but smooth: voices break, crack, squeak, drop, or leap up at the most inappropriate times. Youngsters are embarrassed when these things happen to them. Parents and friends should not tease boys whose voices misbehave.

Boys have also the problem of ejaculating seminal fluid. They may do this accidentally when they are asleep or intentionally while they are awake. Boys feel guilty and embarrassed after they have done this and are afraid someone will discover the evidence. Wise parents understand. They regard occasionally soiled bed linens as indications that their sons are normal, healthy boys; they are glad that nature is taking its course. The worst thing they could do would be to scold the youngsters or punish them.

The foreskin on the *glans penis* of uncircumcised boys is sometimes troublesome. Most male babies are circumcised soon after they are born; however, a few of them are not.

Uncircumcised boys have hygiene problems created by the foreskin which makes the *glans penis* difficult at times to keep clean and free from irritation. Yet, the *glans penis* must be kept clean for health reasons as well as for personal reasons.

Medical authorities recommend that all male babies be circumcised at birth and that boys who are missed should be circumcised as soon as feasible. Circumcision is a simple, harmless operation that involves small risk and only a little special care.

Adolescent boys should be examined by a physician to be sure their reproductive equipment is normal. The most common defect is failure of the testicles to descend fully into the scrotum. *Undescended testicles* are usually detected before adolescence; sometimes, however, they are overlooked.

Teen-age boys worry about their relative adequacy as males. The doctor may help them feel better about themselves by reassuring them after the examination that they are normal, healthy, masculine young men.

Review of major points

1. Rapid growth during preadolescence has special meanings.
2. Boys and girls mature at different rates.
3. Physical symptoms of sexual maturity include menstruation (girls) and seminal emissions (boys).
4. Adolescent growth patterns tend to confuse boy-girl social relationships.
5. Abnormal rates of maturing may signal trouble.
6. Secondary growth characteristics indicate sexual maturity.
7. Adolescence demands additional attention to cleanliness and personal hygiene.
8. Dental care during adolescence is imperative.
9. Adolescents need minimum schedules for adequate self-maintenance.

10. Parents may help youngsters establish good habits of personal care.
11. Menstruation poses special problems for girls.
12. Boys, too, have special problems.

SUMMARY

This chapter discussed important aspects of growth and development during adolescence and suggested ways in which parents can help their children live successfully through this period of rapid, dramatic change.

The next chapter will discuss emotional problems of adolescence and suggest ways parents may help their youngsters face these problems realistically.

Chapter 3

How Adolescents Feel about Themselves

A MIDDLE-AGED mother of two teen-agers was complaining about her husband during a recent marriage counseling session. "He's very immature," she said. "He's moody and irritable. He gets excited and loses his temper over nothing at all. He gets angry over little things, and then he sulks. I never have the faintest idea what I have said or done to upset him. Honestly, Dr. Glover, sometimes I think I'm married to an *adolescent!"*

Adolescence is a period marked by emotional instability. Everything the lady said about her husband describes the emotional behavior of normal teen-agers: immature, moody, irritable, excitable, temperamental, aggressive or withdrawn, easily upset. Here are a few examples of the kinds of behavior they may display:

Mary became violently angry at her father when he suggested that perhaps she should wear a modest blouse rather than the tight-fitting sweater she was wearing.

John refused to appear in the school play because he was afraid his voice would "crack."

Alice was wandering about the house one Saturday morning very downcast, gloomy, depressed. Her mother asked her what was the matter. Alice answered, "Nothing, Mother. Please leave me alone!" Then she burst into tears and ran into her bedroom, slamming the door behind her. She stayed in her room the rest of the day.

Bill was secretly in love with Joanne but was too shy to talk with her. Joanne stopped Bill in the hall at school one day and asked him to come to a party at her house Friday night. Bill, flustered and embarrassed, blurted out, "I'm going out of town with my father right after school on Friday." Bill was so angry at himself he became ill later and had to be excused from class.

Darlene refused to go onto the stage during assembly to accept her scholarship award. She had overheard a derogatory remark as she walked past a group of girls in the hall. The dean of girls asked her later why she would not go on the stage. Darlene replied, "I don't want that old award!"

Celeste and her sister *Kathryn* were in church with their parents. They whispered to each other briefly and started giggling. Their parents nudged them, warning them to be quiet. Celeste and Kathryn tried to control themselves, but the harder they tried to stop, the more they giggled. Tears rolled down their cheeks; the girls shook with suppressed laughter. Celeste's and Kathryn's parents, embarrassed that the girls were attracting attention and annoying the minister and the congregation, told them to leave. Their mother asked them later what was so funny. Celeste and Kathryn explained, "Oh, it wasn't really funny; we just started laughing and couldn't stop."

Harry was watching the high school football game. The referee made a highly questionable decision that resulted in a touchdown for the visiting team. The local cheering section booed lustily. Harry, mild-mannered and easy-going as a rule, leaped from the stands, grabbed the down marker, raced to the end of the playing field and swung the marker viciously at the referee. He missed, fortunately. The principal questioned him later about the incident. Harry said meekly, "I lost my head."

Harriet refused to go with her parents to the Johnsons because these people had embarrassed her. Mrs. Johnson had remarked, when she was a guest in Harriet's home the previous week, "Poor, awkward teen-agers—they're all thumbs." Mrs. Johnson was not referring to Harriet. But Harriet thought she was.

Claude was embarrassed when his mother excused herself from the breakfast table saying, "I must straighten up the house before I get ready for church. I'll have to change the bed linens." Claude blushed and squirmed because he thought the second remark was directed to him. His mother had said the same thing on previous occasions, but he had not taken it personally.

Successful parents do not try continually to suppress their teen-agers' behavior patterns when they seem unstable. Rather, they accept them and try to understand how their youngsters feel. By doing this, they help them outgrow the patterns.

Teen-agers feel uncertain about their "new" faces and bodies. The frustration teen-agers meet trying to understand and accept their new bodies accounts for some of their emotional instability. Adolescents are more aware of their own appearance than other persons. Here, for example, is a description of a typical fourteen-year-old girl preparing for her first date:

Mary Bradshaw sauntered into her bedroom and sat down at the dressing table. She smiled seductively at herself in the mirror, ran a comb lightly through her hair, then picked up a brush and went to work in earnest.

"Wish Mom would let me cut it short," she grumbled. She turned on the make-up lamp and examined her skin in the magnifying mirror. It was clear except for three small, red blemishes near her left cheek.

"Those darned pimples!" she thought. "One yesterday, two more today. Oh, well, guess I'm not too bad off. Just look at poor Zelda—her face is a mess!"

Mary swept back her hair with both hands and held it tightly against her head. "Doris says I'd look like Kim Novak if I cut it." She saw Kim Novak in fantasy. She struck a Kim-like pose and moved close to the mirror for a better look.

"I do have Kim's eyes. . . . And her lips—if I hold my mouth open a little like this. . . . And her chin. But that's not her nose! Her nose is cute. Mine is simply awful. It's so ugly. My nose is simply huge!"

Mary released the grip on her hair and sat up straight. She blinked, frowned, and returned again to reality.

Most teen-agers compare themselves with their friends, with members of their own families, with their favorite movie stars. They worry about the size and shape of their nose, chin, mouth, ears, eyes, eyebrows, teeth, chest, hips, arms, legs, hands, fingers and nails. They worry about the blemishes on their skin, the curl (or lack of it) in their hair, the pitch and quality of their voice, and a thousand other painful details.

Many boys want to improve their physiques. They are quite impressed by professional muscle men such as Charles Atlas, who recalls, "I was a 97-pound weakling." They may go to a gymnasium to build up their muscles or set up exercising equipment in the garage at home.

Girls want to improve their figures, too. They worry about their weight, measurements, and bust-waist-hip ratios.

Wise parents accept teen-agers' normal interest in their appearance and give them the encouragement and support they need. They reassure them that they are attractive and will become even more attractive as they mature. At the same time, they emphasize the fact, however, that while physical attractiveness is important, it is not as important as good character.

Teen-agers underestimate themselves. Teen-agers are usually overly critical of themselves. Adults who recall their own adolescence remember that they were often self-effacing. A prominent business executive, for example, told me recently how he felt about himself as an adolescent:

When I was thirteen or fourteen years old, I suddenly shot up tall. It seemed no time at all before I had grown from a little boy to a gangling youth. By my sixteenth birthday, I was almost as tall as I am now (six feet, five inches) and I weighed only one hundred forty pounds.

I figured I had a good build for basketball, and so I went out for the team. I made it and became a good player. But even this success didn't keep me from feeling embarrassed at being so tall and skinny.

I remember comparing myself with some of the fellows on the football team, contrasting my long, thin arms and legs with their stocky, muscular ones. I still wanted to be powerful like those lads. I decided to try out for the football team in spite of my toothpick build.

The coach put me on the defensive team—the "scrubs." The varsity squad used us as opponents in practice scrimmages. They ran their offensive plays through us. I mean that literally—*they ran through us.* We were to the varsity football team what a punching bag is to a prize fighter. I got hit so hard, so often, and in so many places that I was black and blue for weeks. I was so stiff and sore I could hardly drag myself out of bed in the mornings.

After a while I decided to abandon football and specialize in basketball, where being tall and skinny was an asset rather than a liability. My decision paid off: I made the all-conference team. Later, I played basketball in college, and then I had four years as a pro.

I shall never forget how, as a teen-ager, I always envied the football players' solid-rock physiques. I always thought of myself as a long straw by comparison. I realize now that I should not have felt inferior because of my body build. I was a late maturer: I reached my full height when I was sixteen years old, but I was still filling out in my late twenties.

Adolescents are very self-conscious. They are really too critical of themselves. I know from my own experiences exactly how they feel.

Parents are wise who do not make an issue, either directly or by implication, of their teen-agers' physiques.

For example, they do not tag youngsters with nicknames that suggest unusual physical traits: "Skinny," "Tubby," "Mooseface," "Beanpole," "Toughy," "Handsome," "Beautiful," "Stubby," "Porky," "Fats," "Lard Bucket," "Tiny," "Pimples." Youngsters get plenty of ribbing about their appearance from their peers. They can usually take teasing from friends, but they do not deserve to be teased by parents.

Parents are wise, too, who tolerate their adolescents' normal postural changes. They do not nag at them: "Stand up straight!" "Hold you shoulders up and back!" "Sit up, for heaven's sake—don't slump!" "Go look at yourself in the mirror . .. you look terrible!" And so on, *ad infinitum.* Successful parents know that a positive approach to helping teen-agers brings better results. They provide facilities and equipment for good grooming and encourage teenagers to impose upon themselves their own standards. They know that teen-agers grow out of limp, slouching, slumping postures, as a rule, if parents do not make an issue of them.

Teen-agers feel insecure. Adolescents suffer feelings of insecurity more often than members of other age groups. This fact is due in part to the youngsters' developmental stage: they are in a difficult position in life, being no longer children but not yet adults.

Feelings of insecurity are often difficult to identify and interpret because they are intangible. Yet they are plentiful during adolescence, as any truthful teen-ager will readily admit.

Teen-agers may reveal feelings of insecurity and in-adequacy with such comments as these: "Am I worth putting up with?" "Will I be successful at anything?" "Will I get married?" "Will I be able to hold a job?" "Am I wasting my time going to school?" "Am I learning any-thing in school that will help me in later life?"

Teen-agers express deep feelings of insecurity often through symptoms of nervousness. For example, they may be easily excited. They may "blow their tops" over matters that seem quite trivial to adults. They may worry about little things that will probably have no bearing on their lives two years hence. They may act impulsively, do things without thinking and regret later having done them. They may bite their fingernails, chew their lips, pick at facial blemishes, clear their throats too frequently, cough unnecessarily, blink too often and too dramatically. All teenagers do not have such symptoms; indeed, some youngsters have none of them. Yet most adolescents reveal anxieties and inner tensions by displaying one or more nervous habits.

Many teen-agers feel lonesome much of the time, even when they are with others. They feel that they are different, that there is perhaps something suspect about themselves. They distrust even their own feelings about themselves. They wonder sometimes whether they are normal; in fact, many teen-agers believe they are not normal. Many youngsters doubt that they are wanted or accepted by their peers, even though there may be no reasonable grounds for doubt.

Teen-agers are quite sensitive about other people's attitudes toward them. More accurately, they are overly sensitive to what they imagine others think of them. Their feelings are hurt easily and often; they are vulnerable to attack, real or imagined.

Many teen-agers, to avoid being hurt, refuse to take chances. They sidestep situations when they think they may fail. The thought of being humiliated by failure is very painful. This fear, which is usually quite irrational, prevents many teen-agers from developing their natural abilities and creative talents. Thus, a brilliant boy may do mediocre work in school because his buddies are mediocre students, and he is afraid they will not like him if he is different. He is afraid of being a social failure. A gifted girl, equally fearful, makes all A's in school to please her mother. Aptitude tests suggest that she is talented in mathematics; yet she avoids mathematics courses because she is afraid she cannot make A's in them. She is afraid she will lose her mother's love if she makes a B.

Many teen-agers worry about their ideals. Ideals mean different things to different adolescents: to some they mean standards that must be met, and to others they mean standards that cannot be met. Teen-agers regard ideals generally in terms of function; that is, they think ideals mean either doing or not doing certain things (behaving oneself, not getting into trouble, not necking or petting too much).

Many teen-agers chide themselves for failing to live up to their ideals, which are sometimes unreasonably high. They feel they have disappointed their parents, their friends, and themselves. They suffer feelings of guilt because they have not tried hard enough to be responsible, thoughtful and careful. Most of them think they should do better.

Parents may help teen-agers who suffer unduly from guilt feelings over ideals by accepting their supposed weaknesses and by reassuring them that they are loved in spite of what they have done or failed to do.

Teen-agers escape reality often through daydreams. Most adolescents daydream a lot. Daydreaming means escape from reality through fantasy. It differs from constructive use of imagination in that daydreaming is uncontrolled.

Daydreaming provides temporary relief from frustrations growing out of conflicts that cannot be readily resolved. Sex, love, and marriage provide an example. Boys and girls who have reached puberty are biologically able to mate and to procreate; yet the demands of the culture force most of them to postpone extensive physical intimacies for several years. The youngsters withdraw, therefore, from a reality that is frustrating and daydream instead about members of the opposite sex.

Disappointment in one's physique leads also to daydreams. Jimmy, for example, is short and thin; he feels inferior because of his size. In his fantasies, he is a large, muscular hero whom boys fear and girls admire. Hazel, a large, heavy, unattractive girl, daydreams of herself as being small, impish, cute. Girls envy her, boys adore her.

Parents who understand teen-agers permit them to daydream. They do not interrupt them or insist that they "snap out of it." They know that daydreaming serves a useful purpose as a safety valve to frustrated emotions. They know too that excessive daydreaming disappears ordinarily after adolescence.

Teen-agers escape reality sometimes through over-activity. Some teen-agers are always on the go. They are seldom home because they are too busy elsewhere. They go frequently to parties, dances, beaches, pools. They go to high school athletic contests at home and away. They race off with their friends at almost any hour, day or night. They cannot settle down.

Overactivity appears to be the opposite of daydreaming; yet its purpose is essentially the same: to escape frustrations that reality creates. Overactivity takes the place of fantasy. Thus, Virginia is always "bursting with energy," and Vernon "simply never runs down." They are too busy to daydream.

Chronic daydreamers are usually introvertive, while overly active youngsters are usually extrovertive. Introverts turn inward to themselves for relief, while extroverts turn outward to others. Neither introversion nor extroversion is necessarily good or bad; rather, the two patterns are simply opposite ways of reacting to similar stimuli. If you think your teen-agers are either too passive or too active for their own good, you may want to consult your family physician.

Teen-agers escape reality by idolizing people and things. Devotion to music—rock 'n' roll, bop, classical, jazz, or what have you—and to musicians represents another avenue of escape from reality and temporary relief from frustration. Many adolescents lose themselves listening to records.

Devotion to movie stars and television personalities represents similar escape into fantasy. The huge number of best-selling publications (books, magazines, newspaper columns, etc.) about motion picture and television stars testifies to their importance in public fantasy. Most of the fans are young people. A recent study by a motion picture producer revealed, for example, that 84 percent of all movie theater tickets are sold to teen-agers. That figure explains why most so-called adult movies are really designed to appeal to adolescent audiences.

Parents can help teen-agers grow up emotionally. The gloom that engulfs adolescents often leaves parents feeling rather helpless. They wonder whether they can do anything to help their teen-agers grow up. Parents can help teen-agers to live through normal emotional upheavals. Here are some things to do.

1. *Learn the characteristics of adolescents and accept them.* Parents help teen-agers most who understand what they are going through, give them the emotional support they need, and wait patiently for them to enter the next stage of development.

2. *Discover your youngster's strong points, and focus your attention on them.* Talk about your teen-agers' strengths. Be glad they have them. Do not be looking always for their weaknesses. If you see some weaknesses, write them down and file them for a week before you mention them. Give yourself time to gain perspective and to think of possible ways to help your youngsters over come weaknesses or live with them.

3. *Be generous with praise—it works wonders.* Praise creates wholesome, positive feelings in young people and gives them additional self-confidence.

4. *Do not nag.* Teen-agers are often irritable, moody, shy, and withdrawn. It is usually unwise to try to bring them out of it. Nagging at them only makes them angry, and then they feel guilty for being angry. It is usually best to leave them alone. They will eventually grow out of this kind of behavior.

5. *Permit teen-agers release from tension.* Wholesome social activities and conventional entertainment media

(radio, television, motion pictures, record players, etc.) will suffice as a rule to relieve normal tensions.

6. *Provide teen-agers adequate independence.* This means freedom of movement with a minimum amount of adult supervision.

7. *Provide individual teen-agers the privacy they need.*
Every teen-ager should have his (or her) own room if possible. If this is not possible, he should have at least a personal area into which no one else intrudes: a portion of a room; a closet; a chest of drawers; somewhere else that private possessions may be kept with the assurance that no one will bother them.

8. *Be available to teen-agers when they need you.* Develop "big ears" that listen willingly when youngsters tell you their troubles. Do not pry into teen-agers' affairs unless you are invited to pry. Even then, you will probably be more valuable as a most willing listener.

9. *Be aware of serious emotional disorders in some adolescents.* It is usually safe to assume that an individual's behavior is normal. Do not forget, however, that the rate of emotional disturbance and mental illness zooms upward during adolescence. Schizophrenia, for example, becomes apparent more frequently during adolescence than any other period of life. Suicides and suicidal accidents occur rather frequently among teen-agers, especially those who seem to be depressed. Be alert, therefore, to the possibility that adolescents who behave strangely or inappropriately may need psychiatric help.

Review of major points
1. Adolescence is marked by emotional instability.
2. Teen-agers feel uncertain about their "new" faces and bodies.
3. Teen-agers underestimate themselves.
4. Teen-agers feel insecure.
5. Teen-agers are generally quite sensitive about other people's attitudes toward them.
6. Many teen-agers worry about their ideals.

7. Teen-agers escape reality often through daydreams.
8. Teen-agers escape reality sometimes through over-activity.
9. Teen-agers escape reality often by idolizing people and things.
10. Parents can help teen-agers grow up.

SUMMARY

This chapter described adolescence as a period of growth and development marked by emotional instability and suggested ways parents can help teen-agers live through it successfully.

The next chapter will analyze the various roles friends play in the lives of teen-agers and suggest ways in which parents may help adolescents establish meaningful friendships.

Chapter 4

Encouraging Wholesome Friendships

"YOUNG ADOLESCENTS," a prominent psychiatrist said recently, "are explorers in search of *themselves.* The goal they seek is elusive because it cannot be seen nor heard nor felt.

"Untrained and inexperienced in the ways of negotiating emotional jungles, these youngsters are afraid. They move forward, sometimes cautiously, sometimes impulsively. Confused at times and bewildered, they never really know that the paths they tread will lead them to the jungle clearing that is marked *Maturity.*

"To face this fearsome excursion entirely alone would be truly dreadful. It would mean suffering in isolation the uncertainties of today and tomorrow. It would mean suffering alone the whiplash of conscience of discovering shocking secrets about self. These kinds of experiences are too devastating for anyone to endure alone.

"Thus, the teen-ager, faced with the painful anxieties of growing up, must share his feelings. He desperately needs someone who accepts him as he is. He needs someone who really understands. In brief, he needs someone who will be his *best friend.* "

Teen-agers need many friends. Teen-agers need boys and girls who, like themselves, are experiencing the dramatic change of life called *adolescence* and the emotional turmoil that accompanies it. Just being near one another helps ease frustrations, relieve tensions, reduce feelings of uncertainty. Young people feel safer when they are with others. They seem to believe that in numbers there is strength. They enjoy the sensation of security that comes of being in a crowd.

The "herd instinct" is more apparent during adolescence than at any other period of life. Every normal youngster wants to find himself; yet he submerges his unique qualities willingly to belong to a group because he is confused and afraid. As an integral part of the group, which is larger and more powerful than himself, he tends to forget, temporarily at least, his fear, his confusion, his feelings of inadequacy.

Adolescence is indeed a period of exploration in search of self. The young adolescent turns gradually away from his parents (who represent authority) and toward persons who, like himself, are experiencing dramatic bodily changes and emotional upheavals. The typical adolescent does not turn his back on his parents once and for all. He still confides in them, but not as frequently as before. He confides in his friends much more because he thinks they really understand him.

Teen-agers need one or more best friends. The best friend plays an important role in the life of the normal young teen-ager. This person (or persons, for most youngsters have several best friends) is someone outside the family with whom the teen-ager shares his thoughts and feelings. This youngster cares more for the teen-ager than just liking him; he accepts him unreservedly as he is. This is the person to whom the teen-ager tells his troubles, his triumphs, his innermost secrets. Next to his own parents (and, in some cases, even before his own parents), the best friend is usually the most important person in the teen-ager's life. This relationship is essential for the teen-ager: without his best friend he may try to meet life's problems alone. He cannot accomplish this task satisfactorily by himself unless he possesses unusually vast inner resources.

How do young adolescents become best friends? Such intimate friendships emerge naturally from the social soil as seeds sprout naturally from the earth. Becoming best friends is usually a matter of permitting human nature to take its course. The environment has much to do with it. Best friends live in the same neighborhood as a rule, and their parents enjoy equal social status. Best friends usually go to the same school and are often in the same class. They have several similar interests. Best friends are usually the same sex; however, as adolescents grow older, they select members of both sexes as best friends. Two youngsters who have allied themselves as best friends seek to satisfy their deep need for security through sharing. They enjoy each other's trust and confidence. They lend each other encouragement and moral support. They enjoy each other's successes and suffer each other's failures. They joke and laugh together and tease each other. They argue for fun. Sometimes they get angry, but they usually recover quickly and remain best friends.

Best friends are like married couples in some ways. They are jealous of each other's attention, for example, when an outsider tries to intrude. They are proud to be seen together because they hold each other in high esteem. They complement each other's needs; indeed, when they are apart, they feel often as if they are incomplete persons. They may reflect this feeling in their changed behavior. Parents say, "Our teen-ager is a different person when he is separated from his best friends."

Strange combinations of individuals emerge sometimes as best friends. These remarkable alliances grow out of emotional needs; they are certainly not based on reason. Such emotional needs are usually transitory; the stimulation provided by the best friend makes them run their course rather quickly. Thus, adolescents remain best friends only as long as the emotional support that the relationship lends is really necessary and helpful, or until another person comes along who gives this support more effectively. In either case, the alliance comes to a natural end eventually.

The telephone is in effect an extension to best friends. The family telephone plays an important role in the process of transferring dependency relationships from parents to peers. It is not news that teen-agers—especially the younger ones—attach themselves to the telephone and chatter with best friends by the hour if they are permitted to do so. There is nothing abnormal about this practice; on the contrary, it is part of the over-all pattern of gaining independence.

Teen-agers' devotion to the telephone reflects overwhelming feelings of loneliness and overdependence on age-mates for emotional support. It reveals also feelings of personal inadequacy, lack of self-confidence, and low self-esteem. Being almost constantly in touch with friends is imperative; accomplishing this by telephone is the next best thing to doing it in person. Thus, using the telephone too often and too long (by adults' standards) fits into the total scheme of things for the adolescent.

Telephone rules should be formulated by family conference. Parents complain that teen-agers use the telephone too much. They are usually right. Adjustments must usually be made to insure equitable use of the family telephone. Many parents and teen-agers work out rules and regulations by which they abide. They must do this when there is only one telephone in the house; otherwise, a person calling when a teen-ager is at home is likely to get a busy signal.

Rules must be fully acceptable to every member of the household if they are to be effective. Rules regarding use of the telephone should be formulated, therefore, in a family council. Teen-agers in some families restrict their telephone conversations to certain hours of the day or evening. Some youngsters limit the number of calls they make and the length of each call. Some adolescents ask their friends to telephone during certain hours and to refrain from calling at all other times except in case of emergency. (Naturally, the word emergency means different things to different people.)

Some parents ignore the values of the family council and dictate rules regarding use of the telephone. An authoritarian stand is sometimes necessary to clear an otherwise foggy atmosphere. This practice is short-sighted, however, when used too frequently. Household rules—including those regarding the telephone—are more reasonable, more acceptable, and better obeyed when everyone in the family has a hand in formulating them. Oddly enough, teen-agers impose harsh rules upon themselves that they would resent having imposed by autocratic adults.

A few parents have a second telephone installed in the home for their teen-agers. They say it is a good investment because it avoids arguments and provides them ready access to their own phone, eliminating the need to compete for it. There are apparent advantages in this arrangement; yet there may be dangers as well. Should adolescents have private telephones and use them without restraint or parental supervision? I doubt it. Most parents will give this problem careful thought before they give teen-agers sole custody of a telephone.

Teen-agers are sometimes hostile toward parents. Most parents want to help their youngsters grow up, and they do help them. Helping adolescents requires accepting many behaviors that one would ordinarily correct in younger children. For example, adolescents ignore many suggestions parents make "for their own good." They show a remarkable lack of appreciation for things their parents do for them at considerable expense and sacrifice.

Parents who understand adolescents realize that the thirteenth, fourteenth, and fifteenth years of life are perhaps the roughest ones. These years mark a period of stress for most youngsters in relation to their parents and to other members of the family. During these years, boys and girls want to grow up, to be independent; yet they do not have the maturity, the inner resources, or the knowledge to sustain themselves in modern America. Faced with this dilemma, young adolescents tend, as we have already seen, to rebel against parents and to turn to their peers for support. It is not until they are sixteen or seventeen years old that most teen-agers are mature enough to regard their parents and other members of the family as normal human beings who have feelings and rights as important as their own.

Teen-agers use parents and best friends as confidants. In view of young adolescents' normal feelings of hostility toward their parents, it is surprising indeed that parents continue to hold the most prominent position as teen-agers' confidants. The popular belief that adolescent rebellion means inevitable chaos for parent-child relationships has been shattered by several recent studies. Dr. Harold J. Reed, reporting on research conducted at the University of California at Los Angeles (UCLA) says, "Most teen-agers confide *in their parents,* especially in their mother; and they confide frequently also in friends. This pattern of confiding persists throughout high school, from the ninth grade through the twelfth. Only a few more twelfth-graders than ninth-graders confide in friends."

Dr. Reed's findings at the high school level almost duplicate the findings of a nationwide study conducted at the college level by the author. College freshmen and sophomores (seventeen-, eighteen-, and nineteen-year-olds) who were neither engaged nor married used their own mother most often as confidant. Next in frequency was girlfriend, then boyfriend, and then father in fourth place. More than eighty per cent of all the personal confidences these students shared were directed to parents and friends. The pattern of relying mainly on mother and girlfriend persisted in all categories of students except one: male students who were married and going to school took their problems to father more often than to mother; and, of course, girlfriend was replaced by spouse—who, it may be presumed, was previously the young man's favorite girlfriend.

You, as a parent, rank probably at or near the top as your teen-agers' confidant, especially if you are their mother. Yet your youngsters probably confide almost as frequently in their best friends. This knowledge has one important implication: you should be very aware of the kinds of persons your teen-agers choose as best friends.

Take special interest in your teen-agers' best friends.

Parents like their teen-agers' best friends as a rule and accept them almost as if they were members of the family. This attitude helps adolescents grow up, and it helps parents communicate with their teen-agers.

Parents may dislike some individuals whom their offspring select as best friends. Try as they may, they cannot honestly approve their youngsters' choices; consequently, they do not accept these friends in the fullest sense, but they may tolerate them.

Having reservations about some teen-agers is certainly understandable. Most parents regard their own youngsters very highly and set high standards for them. They want their children to do their best—to fulfill their highest potential. They do not want them to fall in with bad company—with youngsters whose moral standards seem much too low and whose behavior patterns reflect these low standards.

How serious a problem are best friends whom you feel are undesirable? It all depends. They will not necessarily leave indelible marks on youngsters' character; yet the danger must not be minimized. If your teen-agers' character rests on solid, firm foundations that were built with considerable care during the formative years (birth to six years old), questionable friends are not likely to influence them very much. Your youngsters will probably recognize character weaknesses; they are not likely to admire these weaknesses or adopt them.

Young people who are sure of themselves are not ordinarily searching for someone to emulate; consequently, they need not be protected or carefully guided in choosing companions. Teen-agers who, on the other hand, are highly suggestible, readily influenced, and easily led need strong parental guidance to establish worthwhile friendships. They must be guided to companions who will lead them in the right direction, not the wrong one.

A few parents encourage their teen-agers to be companions with all kinds of boys and girls, including those of questionable character. They do this on the theory that knowing all kinds of people prepares their offspring more effectively for adulthood. In other words, they want them to be as sophisticated as possible in human relations rather than to remain naïve. There is undoubtedly some merit to this point of view; youngsters may learn important lessons from character deviates. In my opinion, however, the normal teen-ager gains little as a rule from associating with people who suffer personality disturbances or character disorders. Furthermore, there is always an outside chance that he may be harmed by associating closely with them.

Encourage teen-age friendships that are wholesome and constructive. What may parents do to encourage teen-agers to cultivate wholesome, constructive friendships and to eliminate those that are definitely undesirable? There are several things you can do. You must do them subtly, however, because adolescents tend to reject direct encouragement or direct interference by parents.

Meet your teen-agers' friends, if at all possible, and get to know them well. Treat them as real persons who deserve your consideration and respect. Do not criticize them or indicate in any way that you think there might be something wrong with them or with teen-agers in general. *Remember youngsters' names, and use them.* Nothing is more flattering or reassuring to young people than to hear adults call them by name, showing that they are interested in them. It is always a mistake to ignore individual identities. No one enjoys being known only as "You."

Give every youngster maximum opportunity to prove himself worthwhile. Do not jump to the conclusion that just because an adolescent looks different or unusual he is necessarily the wrong companion for your teen-ager. It is unwise to pass judgment on any individual without knowing a lot about him. If your early impressions of a youngster are negative, reserve judgment until you know him better.

Make it easy for your teen-agers' friends to come into your home. If you want your youngsters' friends to come to your home, your inner feelings of acceptance and warmth will probably show through. Doing little things for teen-agers, such as serving refreshments occasionally or asking them to stay for lunch, makes them sure they are welcome and wanted. Helping someone else's offspring feel secure is admittedly not your main function as a parent; yet every adult is morally obligated to help all youngsters whenever he can.

Know the parents of your teen-agers' best friends. Chances are you know them already, for they are probably your own friends and neighbors. Assuming, however, that you do not know them, you might arrange to participate in community gatherings (at church, for example, or at school) that they attend regularly. After you have met them casually, you may want to invite them to your home. One good method of getting to know parents better is to ask them to help you supervise (as chaperons) a teen-age social event that your youngsters and theirs will attend. You will meet them on informal terms this way and gain new insights into their children—your teen-agers' best friends.

If a best friend has an unwholesome influence on your teen-ager, see that the relationship is terminated. The task of terminating a close friendship between adolescents without damaging your relationship with your teen-ager is a most delicate one indeed. A positive but indirect approach to the problem is generally best. Encourage your youngster to recognize the dangers of associating closely with this individual. Try to get him to terminate the alliance in his own way. This approach may take more time and patience on your part but will probably prove to be more effective in the long run because it permits your youngster to feel that he, not you, makes the final decision. If you use the opposite approach (that is, if you intervene directly and order the alliance dissolved), you may jeopardize your relationship with your teen-ager. He is trying to establish his own independence and will probably resent blunt, authoritarian action on your part.

Another approach to terminating an unwholesome alliance is to encourage strongly a friendship that you think is desirable. This method, too, must be applied subtly rather than directly. The main obstacle is that teen-agers and their parents do not always agree on who would make a "desirable" best friend.

A time may come when you will simply have to exercise your parental authority directly to terminate an unwholesome friendship. This method is not generally recommended; yet it is definitely the right one in some cases. Teen-agers may, for example, select unsavory characters as companions for the sole purpose of testing their parents' love. If the parents are too relaxed and do not interfere in these shady relationships, the children conclude that the parents do not care enough about them to be bothered. They may involve themselves too deeply with these companions and get into trouble, thereby forcing their parents to pay more attention to them.

The ideal relationship between teen-agers and parents with reference to best friends manifests itself when parents are permissive enough to let their youngsters choose their own friends but are authoritarian enough to interfere when they make choices that are obviously bad ones. This kind of arrangement helps adolescent boys and girls know that their parents still love them and are definitely interested in their welfare.

If teen-agers have no close friends, consider this pattern a symptom of possible personal-social maladjustment. Adolescents who have no best friends are often too dependent on their parents—usually on Mother, since she is ordinarily the youngsters' confidant. Afraid of being hurt in social relationships, they stay at home, clinging psychologically to the parents for protection. In taking this easy way out, they become socially stunted; and if they fail to break out of this pattern of overdependence, they are headed for troubled times.

Parents whose youngsters have no close friends should examine their own relationships with them. Perhaps they are protecting them into much. Perhaps they do not really want them to grow up.

Parents of friendless teen-agers should confer with the youngsters' counselors at school and church. Wise counselors see youngsters objectively in relation to their peers. They may help you guide them to greater personal and social competence.

If your youngster withdraws rather consistently from other people and if his behavior seems strange, unusual, or somewhat bizarre, consult your family physician. He may want to see your teen-ager, or he may suggest that you secure a psychiatric interview for him. It is well to remember that more mental and emotional disorders show up during adolescence than in any other stage of life.

Review of major points

1. Teen-agers need many friends.
2. Teen-agers need one or more best friends.
3. The telephone is in effect an extension to best friends.
4. Telephone rules should be formulated by family conference.
5. Normal teen-agers are sometimes hostile toward parents.
6. Teen-agers use parents and best friends as confidants.
7. Take special interest in your teen-agers' best friends.
8. Encourage teen-age friendships that are wholesome and constructive.
9. If a best friend has an unwholesome influence on your teen-ager, see that the relationship is terminated.
10. If your teen-agers have no close friends, you might weigh this as a possible symptom of personal-social maladjustment.

SUMMARY

This chapter described young adolescents' need for many friends, especially best friends, and suggested ways in which parents can help them satisfy this need successfully.

The next chapter will discuss young adolescents' social group relationships and suggest ways in which parents may help their youngsters develop personal-social competencies through social group activities.

Chapter 5

Social Group Relationships

"THE ROOTS OF social adjustment," a noted psychologist said recently, "grow most rapidly during infancy and early childhood. Later, during the latent years and adolescence, the basic social behavior patterns that were established during the formative years are the foundation upon which social competencies are built. Thus, social effectiveness during adulthood depends largely upon the quality of social experiences during the formative years, the latent years, and adolescence."

Parents may do many things to help young adolescents develop personal-social competencies through social group relationships. The suggestions that follow may serve as guidelines in this task.

Recognize the value of social group experiences. The term social group experiences is a broad one that includes everything that happens when people get together. The social group forms spontaneously sometimes, while at other times it must be carefully planned. Social groups vary greatly in size, ranging from three people to an almost unlimited number.

Social group experiences are valuable in many ways for teen-agers. They help them become poised, self-confident, and effective in their relationships with other people. They teach them social responsibility—a sense of duty, fair play, and good sportsmanship. They enhance teen-agers' over-all adjustment to everyday living. They help boys and girls relate themselves to their peers and gain perspective on their own social-sex roles in the culture. They make individuals aware of their own assets and liabilities. They help adolescents differentiate sex roles and feel at ease with members of the opposite sex.

Appreciate young teen-agers' need for social group relationships. Young adolescents—the thirteen-, fourteen-, and fifteen-year-olds—need many social group contacts with their peers. Dr. Remmers' study at Purdue University, which involved thousands of adolescents throughout the United States, emphasized this point:

More than half of the youngsters said they want other people to like them better. (This attitude indicates their readiness to seek out people who will accept them and like them as they are.)

Half of the teen-agers said they want to make new friends. (The easiest way to make new friends is to participate in social group activities.)

Almost half of the teen-agers said they wish they were more popular. (In expressing this wish, they were probably revealing their own feelings of inadequacy and expressing their desperate need for their peers' approval.)

One-fourth of the boys and girls said they often feel unsure of themselves. (Here, too, the teen-age social group should be able to help. Made up of individuals who share similar feelings and drives, the group affords the adolescent security that he may not obtain in any other way.)

One-fourth of the teen-agers said they worry a great deal about trying to live up to the ideals of the group. (The social group competes with—and sometimes replaces —the family unit as the main source of ideals and standards for behavior of its members. Therefore, teenagers are usually quite sensitive to the ideals of the group.)

More than one-fifth of the youngsters said they want to feel more important to their own group and to society. (This attitude indicates teen-agers' deep longing for "a place in the sun." It implies also their readiness to grow socially before they move beyond the family group into the wider community.)

Thus, adolescents reach out beyond the home to other persons and institutions in search of themselves. They need desperately to be wanted, to be appreciated, to be recognized. They need to be valued, to be sought, to be loved.

They seek security in friends their own age; finding it, they enhance their own personal-social growth.

Understand the characteristics of small, informal social groups. Young teen-agers organize themselves usually somewhat spontaneously into small, informal social groups, or clusters, or cliques. These groups include members of one sex only—either boys or girls—until the youngsters are fifteen or sixteen years old, when the groups become heterosexual. Group members are usually about the same age. They live in the same neighborhood as a rule, and their parents enjoy approximately the same socio-economic status. The groups are small, being composed ordinarily of three to ten members.

Here are some representative statements by young teen-agers about their own small, informal groups:

RONALD, FOURTEEN YEARS OLD: Five of us boys live on the same street. We do everything together. We have been playing together since we were kids, so I guess doing everything together now is just sort of natural. We like to play baseball and touch [football], and we go to the movies together on weekends. We go fishing sometimes.

BETTY, FOURTEEN YEARS OLD: Nora, Connie, Janice and I go around together because we live close to one another and because we have a lot in common. We are all in the ninth grade at Pasteur [a junior high school], and we have been friends a long time. When we are together—usually at someone's house—we talk a lot and help each other with problems, such as how to get along better with our parents and our teachers. We talk about how to dress, and how to use make-up and things like that. We don't talk much about boys.

MARTHA, FIFTEEN YEARS OLD: The kids I run around with all live in our neighborhood—except one boy, Geoff, who lives in [another section of town]. There are eight of us—four boys and four girls. We always go places together. We usually walk to school together.

Sometimes we eat lunch together. We always stop at Maxie's [a malt shop near the high school] on the way home. After school, we usually hang around together at someone's house an hour or so and play records and talk a lot. Sometimes we dance, but not often. We almost always go to the school dance together on Friday nights, and we sometimes go to a movie on Saturday night. We have a lot of fun. I enjoy being with these kids very much. I forgot to mention that besides us eight regulars, there are four more kids who go with us sometimes, but not often. I think I am lucky to be living in such a friendly neighborhood.

Members of small, informal groups demonstrate their friendship and loyalty to one another in ways that sometimes make parents watch and wonder. For example, they exchange articles of clothing—sweaters, coats, hats, shirts, skirts, shoes, socks, jewelry. They wear these articles whether they fit or not; in fact, the worse the apparel fits, the more apparent that it belongs to a friend. That makes it even better. Group members demonstrate their unity continually by wearing an identifying bit of clothing, such as a bright yellow dinghy cap, or green shoelaces, or flaming red socks, or a purple peasant scarf. Girls in a group may wear the same hairdo and match one another's appearance in other ways. Thus, young adolescents tend to sacrifice their individuality to attain *uniqueness as a group.*

Loyalty to the small, informal social group grows rapidly and appears at times to replace loyalty to the family. This transfer of loyalty from family to group is usually superficial and transitory. It resolves itself ordinarily in a couple of years or when the members are sixteen or seventeen years old. During the intervening period, however, teen-agers vacillate between loyalty to group and loyalty to parents.

Teen-agers are usually quite secretive about their goings-on during this phase and seldom confide in their parents or in other adults. They feel sometimes that parents are impossible old fogies who do not understand how it feels to be young and adventuresome.

The family telephone becomes a serious bone of contention during this period, for it provides means by which youngsters may contact their buddies from within the confines of the "old folks home."

Recognize possible dangers in small, informal groups. Being a member of a small, informal, closely knit group has some definite, positive values for young teen-agers; yet it poses some possible disadvantages.

Advantages: Being a member of a small, informal social group provides companionship and feelings of security; makes the individual feel important to other youngsters; gives the young teen-ager status among his age-mates as one who "belongs"; relieves the youngster of excessive egocentricity by encouraging him to think less in terms of "I," "me," and "mine," and more in terms of "we," "us," and "ours"; provides opportunities to contribute to the welfare of others and to be recognized by peers for doing so; gives him practice at getting along with others; and teaches him to help make group decisions and to abide by them.

Disadvantages: As a member of a small group, the young teen-ager may become *too* loyal to the group, exclude his parents as confidants, and ignore other teen-agers who might be excellent companions; develop hostile attitudes toward other persons because they are outside the group; conform to group pressures and expectations to the point of denying his own uniqueness; inflict emotional injury, intentional or not, upon youngsters who are excluded from the group; do things that are immoral or illegal to win group approval.

The most common criticism of small groups or cliques is this: In their efforts to become "exclusive," "unique," and "the very best," some small groups make their members snobbish. Parents must recognize snobbery in some groups and warn their youngsters against falling into the pattern. Nobody likes a snob, whether he is an adult or a teen-ager.

Help your teen-ager grow up by cooperating with him and his friends. Parents feel generally that the small social group poses a threat to their authority when their own teen-ager is a member. The youngster may become less communicative with his parents, being secretive especially when they ask about his friends. Some parents become quite upset at their teen-ager's unexplained silence and, without thinking through the reasons for his behavior, attack his relationship to his friends in much the same manner they would attack a small fire, putting it out with whatever means are available before it has a chance to spread and cause extensive damage. This approach is obviously wrong and can lead to serious trouble.

Parents who understand teen-agers are not threatened by adolescent devotion to the small group. They know this phase will pass, just as other phases before it passed. Rather than fight it, they make the best of it; and by doing so, they help their teen-agers grow up.

Here are some things you might do to help your young teen-ager and his friends benefit most from group relationships:

Let your youngster know that his friends are welcome in your home. Of course, you must establish reasonable limits and enforce them.

Make your home physically attractive. Teen-agers are more sensitive than young children and adults are about the home's appearance. They may work hard to improve its appearance if they are encouraged to do so.

Make yourself attractive. Adolescents are overly sensitive about their own appearance and project these feelings onto others, especially their own parents. You cannot always expect to please teen-agers' tastes—nor should you even try; yet they will admire you more if you dress neatly and look "sharp."

Respect your youngsters' friends. Respect teen-agers as you respect grown-up persons—parents, for example. Give them the same considerations you would like them to give you. They will usually return your respect and consideration in kind. As one parent put it, "We get back from our young people just about the same kind of treatment we give them."

Provide home recreational materials that teen-agers enjoy. Examples: record player, television set, ping-pong table, card table and cards. Most adolescents enjoy listening to records, dancing occasionally, watching their favorite television programs together, having bull sessions, playing cards, and many other activities. These kinds of recreation are usually available in the home and do not necessarily incur additional expense.

Let adolescents choose their own activities as long as their choices are reasonable. When you are in doubt about the wisdom of teen-agers' choices, suggest substitute activities. Make such suggestions painlessly, without a note of criticism. For example: "Perhaps you would have more fun doing . . ." "Perhaps you folks would like to ..." "Perhaps you would rather . . . than . . .; it's a lot more fun." When things are going well, however, it is usually better to leave well enough alone.

Help young teen-agers with planned social activities. Carefully planned activities require more parental assistance than informal get-togethers that occur among young adolescents day by day. Parties at home, swimming and skating parties, picnics, barbeques, and movie parties are among the most popular planned activities.

A typical planned social activity that involved thirteen-and fourteen-year-old boys and girls is described by the mother of one of the girls:

Mary came to me with a problem. She said she and her friends wanted to have a party at our house and invite some boys from their ninth grade class at school. I was a bit hesitant at first because Mary had just recently turned fourteen years old. Frankly, I wondered whether she and her friends were becoming boy-crazy. However, I went along with the idea and agreed to call each girl's mother and give the party my blessing.

The girls, five of them in all, got together several times after school and made plans. The most important problem was deciding which boys to invite. Each boy had to be acceptable to all five girls, as there were to be no dates or pairing-off. When the final list was made up, I called each boy's mother and explained the girls' plans.

The girls issued their invitations verbally, in person, at school. Fortunately, all of the boys accepted, although I'm sure they weren't as enthusiastic as the girls expected them to be.

The girls planned the activities for the party. I thought they were appropriate, and I agreed to them. They also selected the refreshments and prepared them under my watchful eye.

Mrs. Sorenson, mother of Paul, volunteered to bring all five boys in her car and to take them home after the party. She also volunteered to stay for the party and help me—an offer that I readily accepted.

The party went off quite smoothly. The boys and girls all seemed to enjoy themselves. We stuck with the mixer-type games that were easy to do because all the guests could take part in them at the same time.

Most important of all were the refreshments. They really went over big. I think this was because they were simple and the kinds of things that teen-agers like best. And there was *plenty to eat*

At the end of the party, the boys policed up the living room, which I appreciated very much. This was Mrs. Sorenson's idea, and the boys cooperated. They seemed to enjoy picking up stray items as much as any other game at the party.

Shortly after ten o'clock, Mrs. Sorenson loaded all the boys into her car and took them home. My husband, accompanied by Mary, drove the girls home.

Perhaps the most striking element in this mother's account is the spirit of cooperation that prevailed among the young teen-agers and the parents. Young folks get an idea sometimes and ask their parents' help, only to have the idea rejected at once: the parents refuse to discuss the proposal; they do not want to be bothered. This attitude invites trouble, for it tends to alienate parents from teen-agers. Parents who do this are probably in the minority. Most parents are genuinely interested in their youngsters' welfare and are willing to cooperate. They explore the possibilities of any reasonable idea their children present, and if the idea is a feasible one, they help them carry it out.

Follow sound guidelines to successful group social experiences for young adolescents. Specifics vary among situations, but here are some guidelines to consider when you help young adolescents plan successful social group activities.

Plan social events with considerable care and much attention to details. Do this, and social events will go off so well they will appear to be taking care of themselves. If, on the other hand, an event is not planned carefully, things may get out of hand.

Plan young people's social activities ordinarily for weekends and holidays. This policy is especially important when school is in session. Boys and girls who must go to school the next morning should avoid undue excitement and get enough sleep. When schools are not in session (during summer vacation, for example), it is still better as a rule to schedule social events on weekends and holidays because many boys and girls have part-time jobs or duties at home to perform during the work week.

Schedule social activities in the late afternoon and early evening whenever feasible rather than at night. Young adolescents' social affairs should not be permitted to run far into the night. It is usually better to start them early and end them early. Getting youngsters home early reflects good parental judgment and complies with the spirit of curfew regulations that exist in many communities.

Girls should take the initiative ordinarily in planning

social affairs and decide which boys shall attend. This pattern reflects the greater maturity of the girls as well as the social expectations of the culture.

Each girl should be given the opportunity to invite the boy of her choice if possible, even though there is to be no pairing-off. One boy may be the first choice of two or more girls; the better solution may be, therefore, that the girls agree unanimously on the list of boys to be invited.

Guests of both sexes should be approximately the same age. Allowance must be made, however, for the greater maturity of girls; consequently, some of the boys may be one, two, or even three years older than the girls.

Limit the guests to a reasonable number. The number of young teen-agers to invite to a social affair depends primarily upon the amount of space available. If your house is small, the guest list must be correspondingly brief — unless you have a large yard or garden that accommodates more during the out-door season. The best general guide is to invite as many guests as you and your youngsters feel would fit comfortably into the facilities. Do not overload your home with guests whom you cannot accommodate satisfactorily. On the other hand, do not limit the number of guests so drastically that they fan to constitute a group.

Games and other group activities should be carefully I planned. Activities should involve all guests at the same time at this age level, and there should be enough different kinds of planned activities to preclude monotonous repetition and consequent loss of interest.

Refreshments should be the kinds young adolescents would buy if they had complete freedom of choice. Examples: hamburgers, hot dogs, soft drinks, milk, malteds, hot chocolate, ice cream, doughnuts, cupcakes, cake, and others. Refreshments should be easy to prepare, easy to serve, and easy to consume without leaving too much debris.

Parents should provide transportation for young teen-agers under certain conditions. Examples: When young-sters must travel a considerable distance, when undue hazard exists, when the weather is bad, and when the social event occurs at night.

Few young adolescents are licensed to drive a car; therefore, parents must be sure they get to and from their social affairs safely. This is not the responsibility of the hostess, but it is a problem she must consider.

Parents of guests should transport them or make arrangements to have a responsible adult do it. Parents who live in the same neighborhood and whose adolescents are good friends take turns sometimes driving them places. This arrangement saves everyone time, energy, and expense.

Young teen-agers should always be transported by adults to social events that occur at night. Older teen-agers can usually take care of themselves quite handily after dark; younger ones, however, should not be permitted out at night either alone or in groups without adult protection and supervision.

Adults in addition to the parents of the host or hostess should be present. These persons should chaperon and help out, but they should not try to run the show. One adult (preferably a parent) for each six or eight youngsters should suffice.

Education and training in good manners should be an integral part of every social affair. This objective may be accomplished subtly and indirectly by making good manners inherent in the activities. A good example: Putting the party area back in good order, as the boys did at Mary's party.

The hostess and her parents should be on hand through-out the affair and especially conspicuous during the period of departure. Each guest should have the opportunity to thank the hostess and her parents. This, too, is part of training in good manners. The youngster who says cheer-fully, "Thank you for a wonderful time," or "I enjoyed the party very much; thank you for inviting me," is more likely to be invited again than the one who wanders off without a word of gratitude.

No one should be permitted to linger after a social event or to tarry on the way home. Guests should agree beforehand that they will proceed directly home from a social function unless plans to do otherwise have been approved by their own parents and made known to the hostess's parents. This courtesy is necessary for two reasons: parents should always know where their youngsters are and whom they are with, and young adolescents should not be permitted to wander off alone or in groups without adult supervision.

Some parents are much too permissive about their youngsters' returning home whenever they please. They may think they are doing them a favor by this *laissez-faire* attitude; in reality, they are deceiving themselves. Young teen-agers feel much more secure when their parents take a definite stand on this matter and establish rather exact rules and regulations. They know then just where they stand and what is expected of them. If parents fail to do this, they are probably negligent. In failing to adopt a responsible attitude, they invite serious behavior problems.

Review of major points

1. Recognize the value of social group experiences.
2. Appreciate your teen-ager's need for social group relationships.
3. Know the characteristics of small, informal social groups.
4. Recognize the possible dangers in small group relationships.
5. Help your teen-ager develop social competencies by cooperating with him and his friends.
6. Help young adolescents with planned social activities.
7. Follow sound guidelines to successful social experiences for young adolescents.

SUMMARY

This chapter discussed young adolescents' need for social group relationships, and it suggested ways in which parents can help their youngsters enjoy successful social group experiences.

The next chapter will discuss problems that may arise when young adolescents start dating, and it will suggest ways in which parents can help teen-agers meet these problems successfully.

Chapter 6

Dating Problems

DATING PLAYS AN important role in the process of growing up. Knowing this, most parents want their teen-agers to have many dates. Furthermore, they want them to be successful at dating. This desire to help raises a host of questions such as these: What important values may adolescents derive from dating? When should boys and girls start having dates? How may parents decide when their youngsters are ready to start dating? How may parents help teen-agers develop dating skills? How may parents help youngsters solve such practical problems as how to get a date; how to decline a date; how to act on a date; what to talk about on a date; where to go and what to do on a date; and how to end a date promptly and politely?

Parents formulating their own answers to these questions may find the following suggestions useful.

Recognize the values of dating during adolescence. Dating means fun, excitement, and pleasure for most boys and girls; it means also new experiences, new insights, new understandings. Many parents recognize the lessons teen-agers learn from dating. Here, for example, are some mothers' statements:

"I think dating helps boys and girls develop poise and self-confidence."

"Dating a number of different persons gives a teen-ager a valuable background of social experience."

"Having dates teaches boys and girls to get along together; it helps them understand and adjust to one another."

"Dating makes teen-agers feel more worthwhile—more *grown-up.*"

"Any youngster can have more fun socially if he dates."

"Dating helps boys and girls become more fully aware of the masculine and feminine roles that they must play all their lives."

"Dating is good preparation for marriage. It gives teen-agers the opportunity to observe members of the opposite sex at close range and to evaluate them carefully. Wide experience at doing this helps them choose a marriage partner more intelligently."

"Sometimes dating leads to marriage, which I guess is really the ultimate purpose of dating."

"Teen-agers who don't date are missing a lot."

Let readiness determine when dating shall begin. Adolescent boys and girls should start having dates when they are ready physically, mentally, emotionally, and socially. Readiness for dating can usually be identified.

First, physical maturity is the primary factor in dating readiness; that is, youngsters are not ready to start dating until they have attained sexual maturity. Second, teenagers' mental attitude toward dating is important. Third, a certain degree of emotional stability is necessary for success at dating, this factor being most difficult to measure. Fourth, the background of social experience is important. Young adolescents who for several years have been living, playing, and working with their peers are more likely to be ready for dating than youngsters who have remained aloof, isolating themselves from groups.

How old should an adolescent be before he or she is permitted to have a date? Of course, it is not possible to answer this question directly, because readiness for dating does not correlate closely with chronological age. Most girls attain puberty earlier than boys and are usually more mature both physically and emotionally than boys; therefore, they are usually ready to start dating earlier than boys. This natural difference complicates the lives of teen-agers by mismatching boys and girls in classes at school, where students are grouped primarily according to chronological age. In the seventh and eighth grades, for example, girls tend to be considerably taller and heavier than boys—a difference that is readily apparent even to the most casual observer at a junior high school dance. Many of the girls are ready for boys, but few of the boys are ready for girls.

Studies of adolescent dating behavior furnish some clues to readiness for dating. Drs. Ilg and Ames of the Gesell Institute found, for example, that a few thirteen-year-old girls in their sample were dating quite a lot. About half of the fourteen-year-old girls were going out on dates, and a few of them were going steady. Most of the fifteen-year-old girls were dating, and a few were going steady. All except one of the sixteen-year-old girls were dating, but only a few of them were going steady. As for the boys, the thirteen-year-olds expressed various attitudes toward girls, ranging from boredom to professed interest; however, none of them was dating. About one-third of the fourteen-year-old boys were having dates, and about two-thirds of the fifteen- and sixteen-year-old boys were dating. Approximately one-third of the boys in the Gesell studies postponed dating until they were seventeen years or older.

The Purdue Opinion Panel, directed by Dr. Remmers, reports that 31 per cent of the boys and 40 per cent of the girls in a nationwide survey said they began dating when they were thirteen years old or younger, suggesting that perhaps the boys in the Gesell studies were not quite as precocious socially as the boys in the Remmers study. To Dr. Remmers's question, "At what age do you think teenagers *should* have their first date?", 41 per cent of the boys and girls replied, "When they are thirteen or fourteen years old," and 46 per cent said, "When they are fifteen or sixteen years old." These replies probably reflect the teen-agers' readiness for dating and their parents' attitudes regarding the proper age to begin dating.

Other studies of adolescent dating habits tend to support an important over-all finding of Ilg and Ames and of Remmers: *There is no specific chronological age at which dating should begin.* Some youngsters are ready to have dates when they are twelve years old; others are ready when they are thirteen, fourteen, or fifteen years old or older. To lay down a hard and fast rule, as some parents do, that children must wait for dating until they have reached a certain birthday—the fourteenth, for example, or the sixteenth, or the eighteenth—is usually a mistake. Such a rule has very little scientific evidence to support it; in fact, almost all available evidence suggests the rule is invalid and may be harmful.

Recognize the symptoms of readiness for dating. If readiness for dating, rather than chronological age alone, is to determine when youngsters start dating, parents want to know how to judge a teen-ager's degree of readiness. Several readiness factors that may appear in a youngster's everyday behavior provide useful guidelines. The most common ones are the following:

Postpubescence. The youngster has experienced the growth spurt and has attained sexual maturity.

Age. The girl is ordinarily at least twelve years old; the boy is ordinarily at least thirteen years old.

Awareness. The individual is quite aware of members of the opposite sex. He or she may talk a lot about them.

Attention. The youngster pays special attention to members of the opposite sex, such as walking with them to and from school; talking with them individually or in a group; carrying a girl's books (if a boy); permitting a boy to carry her books (if a girl).

Concern about looks. The rapidly maturing adolescent spends much time before the mirror evaluating his appearance. Looking at himself as a potentially marketable item, he is often unduly upset at what the mirror tells him.

Increased attention to grooming. The youngster tries to improve his appearance by combing and brushing his hair, polishing his shoes, pressing his clothes, and other, similar activities.

Increased attention to personal cleanliness. The youngster who had to be coaxed or bribed to take a bath when he was a child does so voluntarily now and willingly puts on clean, fresh clothing. In a word, he does not want to offend.

Greater courtesy toward members of the opposite sex. Boys who are ready to date do not kick girls' shins or pull their ponytails as they did during preadolescence. Girls no longer hiss and spit like angry, frightened kittens when boys approach; rather, they become sedate.

React wholesomely to your teen-agers' request to start dating. Parents react in a variety of ways to teen-agers' requests to start having dates. Some of them think the requests are ridiculous; others regard them as acts of defiance. These parents say "NO!" as a rule without considering the facts. They may add a few expletives and threats to make sure the youngsters know precisely how they feel. These parents are, fortunately, in the minority.

Most parents respect youngsters' desire to start dating and give the matter the careful consideration it deserves. They do not act surprised or shocked when their teen-agers want to start having dates. They do not make them feel guilty for growing up and having normal, adolescent needs and wishes. They do not tease them, nor shame them, nor embarrass them in other ways. They do not insult them with such ill-considered remarks as, "You're still a baby," or "You're not dry behind the ears," or "Next thing, you'll be wanting to get married!" Such remarks as these are not made in good taste; they serve only to alienate young people from their parents.

It is usually wise to consider beforehand how you will react when your youngster tells you he wants to have his first date. An acceptable answer might be this: "That's nice. Tell me more about it, and then we'll discuss it and decide."

Help your teen-agers develop basic dating skills. Adolescents must have many dates if they are to become socially competent. Getting along together as heterosexual partners is an art, and, like any other art, requires practice to develop skill. The youngster who seldom dates is usually quite unprepared to choose a marriage partner realistically. Yet some parents forbid their teen-agers to date until they are almost old enough to be married. I think they make a serious mistake when they delay dating that long.

Here are some things parents may do to help inexperienced teen-agers start dating and develop dating skills:

Adopt a positive attitude toward dating. Having dates is a normal, wholesome way of developing personal-social skills. Do not try to resist dating per se; if you do, you will fight a losing battle.

Accept readiness as the primary basis for permitting dates. If your youngster is ready to date, let him start dating. If he is not ready, however, do not get worried and start pushing him. Every teen-ager develops readiness at his own rate; your youngster may be a late developer. Urging a teen-ager to date before he is ready makes him feel inadequate.

Expect boys to be a year or two older than girls when they date. Such an age differential tends to equalize the maturity levels of the two sexes. Members of each sex have their own individual growth patterns, however. The chronological ages of partners suggest pairings, therefore, but do not determine them. Minor age differences in either direction are not worth worrying about. Wide differences in age, however, are quite another matter. The adolescent girl who wants to date a man several years her senior should ordinarily arouse parental concern. Young adult males are usually too mature and experienced for the teen-age girl. They may take advantage of her youth-fulness and naïveté.

Do not worry about your young daughter if she appears to be boy-crazy. Being boy-crazy during early adolescence is neither abnormal nor undesirable. Boy-craziness is primarily an early adolescent preoccupation with fantasies about boys. It marks a girl's sudden awakening to her own femininity and her awareness of masculinity in boys, accompanied by a vague, unrealistic idea of what her feelings mean.

The girl who is boy-crazy does not, as a rule, do more than talk a lot and daydream about boys. The next developmental stage brings more mature understanding of members of the opposite sex and more rational thinking about them.

Do not worry too much about crushes. Having a crush is similar to being boy-crazy and should be regarded lightly. Crushes, too, are based primarily on fantasy; thus, they are usually quite incompatible with reality.

Boys and girls have crashes on peers of both sexes and on such unlikely candidates as teachers, ministers, movie stars, television personalities, and their friends' parents. Crushes seem serious to the boys and girls who are having them, yet they vanish quickly as the youngsters become more mature.

Have faith in your teen-agers' character and judgment To have little faith in your children would be to encourage them to misbehave: young people try ordinarily to measure up (or down, as the case may be) to their parents' expectations of them. Statements such as the following when made parenthetically to teen-agers help them regard themselves as levelheaded persons: "I know I can trust you. . . ."; "I'm sure you will do your best. . . ."; "You always think things through carefully and do just what you think is right. . . ."; "I know you always try very hard to be fair to everyone. . . ." Hearing such complimentary remarks makes most teen-agers want to prove the remarks well-founded.

Accept teen-agers; show them that you like them. Many teen-agers feel that adults do not like them, and these feelings are sometimes justified. This negative attitude results in part from teen-agers' guilt feelings over rebelling against adult authority; yet it also results from the fact that many adults—parents included—complain too much about teen-agers and what is wrong with the younger generation. In reality, today's adolescents are not fundamentally different from adolescents of previous generations.

Meet your teen-agers' dates if you can. It is wise to meet your youngster's dates, not just out of curiosity, but to get to know them. It is easy, of course, to meet the daughter's boyfriends, for they must come to the house. It is more difficult to meet the son's girlfriends; nevertheless, it is a good idea to know them if you can.

Leave the way open for youngsters to talk with you about their problems. You are probably willing to listen to your teen-agers; you will reassure them, however, by saying something like this occasionally: "I'm sure you'll get along well, but if ever you're worried, you can always come to me whenever you want to talk about it. I'll try to understand, and perhaps sometimes I can help." It does not hurt your relationship with your teen-agers to "spell out" your willingness and desire to help.

Some parents think if they leave their youngsters to their own devices and stay completely out of their affairs, the future will take care of itself. The future does take care of itself, of course, but it does a poor job of it sometimes without the parents' help.

Give your teen-agers whatever help they need. Young adolescents need help with choice of clothing, appearance, grooming, and other such concerns, especially when they are just beginning to date. Later, they probably will not need help or accept it.

Teach your youngster how to ask for a date, extend an invitation, accept a date or decline one. These skills do not come naturally; they must be learned. Here are some acceptable ways contrasted with unacceptable ways:

Asking and Accepting

BOY:
(preferable) "May I take you to the school dance next Friday night?"
(poor) "What are you doing Friday night?" "Got any

plans made yet for Friday night?" "Are you going to the school dance Friday night?" "I'm looking for a date Friday night. Are you gonna be busy?" "I don't suppose you'd be interested in going with me to the dance Friday night."

GIRL:

(preferable) "Yes. I'd love to go with you." (poor) "Sure. I was wondering when you were gonna ask me."

BOY:

(preferable) "That's great. The dance begins at eight-thirty. I'll call for you at your house at eight-fifteen." (poor) "I'll meet you at the dance [or some place other than the girl's home]."

GIRL:

(preferable) "Swell. I'll be ready."
(poor) "I'll be waiting for you at the curb."

Asking and Declining

BOY:

(preferable) "May I take you to the school dance next Friday night?"

GIRL:

(preferable) "I'm terribly sorry. I've already made other plans."
(poor) "You're too late, buster; you should have asked me sooner." "No, thank you. . . ." [with no explanation.]
"No, thanks—I'm probably the sixth girl you've asked."

BOY:

(preferable) "I'm sorry too." [And then, if he means it—] "Perhaps another time?"
(poor) "Who's taking you?" "Who's the lucky guy?" "What are your 'other plans'?"

GIRL:

(preferable) [If she is interested:] "Yes, I'd like that."
(poor) "Ask me sooner next time."

Inviting and Accepting

GIRL:

(preferable) "Several couples are coming to my home for a dinner-dance Saturday evening, the twenty-first of May. The party will begin at six o'clock. The boys will wear suits. John and Harriet will be there; Bill and Martha; Hank and Louise; Harry and Sally. Will you come as my partner?" [A girl should brief the boy fully on the proposed activity before she invites him to participate in it. She should explain what, when, and where it will be, who will be there, the role of the boy who is being invited. If there is to be a specific kind of dress, this too should be mentioned.]

(poor) "Are you doing anything the night of May twenty-first?" "Would you like to come to my dinner-dance on May twenty-first?"

BOY:

(preferable) "Yes, I'd like very much to come. I'll be there at six o'clock."

(poor) "Okay. But how did you happen to choose me?" [Or some other irrelevant answer.]

Teach your teen-ager how to use the telephone effectively. Many young adolescents need instruction in using the telephone properly to secure and accept dates and to accomplish other social relationships. Here are some suggestions that may help:

Insist that your youngsters always identify themselves when they use the telephone.

Warn them never to put the other party in an embarrassing position by the way they ask questions.

Teach them to avoid wearing out their welcome *via* telephone by calling too often or by talking too long.

Here are some illustrations you might use with your adolescents:

BOY:

(preferable) "Hi, Mary. This is John Smith."

(poor) "Hi, Mary. I'll bet you don't know who this is."
"Hi, Mary. Recognize my voice?" [This is no time for
guessing games.]

BOY:

(preferable) "Mary, may I take you to the prom next
Saturday night?" (poor) "Are you going to the prom
Saturday night?"

BOY:

(preferable) "Hi, Mary. This is John Smith." [Wait for
reply, and then continue:] "If you have five or ten
minutes, I'd like to talk with you about tomorrow's math
assignment."
(poor) "Mary, are you going to be busy a few minutes?"
"Mary, do you have a few minutes to spare?" [Whether
Mary is busy or not, she may or may not want to talk to
John Smith about math.]

*Help your teen-agers decide what to do on a date, if
they need such help.* Young adolescents do not usually
know what to do on a date. If your youngsters have this
problem, you might tell them some of the things other
teen-agers do on dates.

Two factors, time and money, tend to dictate what
most teen-agers do on dates. Drugstore dates for a soda or
a malted milk are the least expensive and the most
popular dating activity among younger adolescents. A
ride in an automobile is inexpensive in terms of gasoline
and oil, but someone must have a car and the driver must
be licensed. Dances and parties at school, at church, and
at home are also quite inexpensive.

Most teen-agers prefer moderately priced dates that are
neither too cheap nor too expensive. Studies show that
going to the movies is easily the most popular dating
activity in the moderate-price range among all age groups.
Next comes parties and dances, and in third place is going
for rides in cars. Other popular activities include attending
commercial sporting events, attending school events for

which a charge is made for admission, and participating in sports. Incidentally, the frequency with which teen-agers participate in sports declines rapidly after the mid-teens; girls then prefer sedentary activities and dancing, and boys tend to follow the girls' lead.

The most expensive kinds of dates involve such elaborate activities as formal dances; dinner-dances in a formal setting, such as a hotel; dinner parties in a high-priced restaurant; dinner-theater and dinner-movie parties; winter sports parties at a resort. The costs of such activities are prohibitive for most teen-agers, at least as general fare. Most adolescents would be hard pressed to pay the immediate costs; in addition, they would have to purchase appropriate clothing and equipment. Only those youngsters who have at their command a considerable amount of money can ever hope, therefore, to keep up with the crowd that dates expensively.

If your teen-agers feel badly because they cannot afford expensive dates, you might console them by saying that the best date is not necessarily the most expensive date.

Answer your youngsters questions about how to act on a date.* Teen-agers who are inexperienced at dating are usually quite worried about how they should act on a date. If your adolescents show this concern, advise them to relax and be themselves—"act natural." In addition, tell them the kinds of behavior boys and girls like most in their dates.

According to objective studies, girls like to date boys who are pleasant, friendly, cheerful, good sports, themselves ("act natural"), clean, neat, well-groomed, well-mannered, polite, masculine, not too self-conscious nor too shy. Boys like to date girls who are pleasant, friendly, cheerful, good sports, themselves, considerate, clean, neat, well-groomed, poised, calm ("not too nervous"), definitely feminine.

Parents must not prejudge teen-agers' dating behavior on the basis of their ordinary, day-to-day behavior in the family. Youngsters who seem self-centered and immature at home may be quite generous, charming, and grown-up when they are on a date, away from the family. Perhaps dating gives them a chance to be themselves.

Teach your teen-agers simple skills in polite conversation. Most adolescents who are inexperienced at dating wonder what they will talk about on a date. They envision themselves spending several anguished hours with a date, not knowing what to say. You may help your teen-agers make conversation a pleasure rather than a problem by suggesting such ideas as these:

Display a friendly interest in your date. Example: "My! What a pretty dress (or sweater, coat, tie, hat, suit, necklace) ; I like it very much."

Ask questions—but only those that are not too personal. Examples: "Did you have an interesting day?" "What are your favorite television shows (or movies, subjects at school, baseball teams, books)?"

Listen intelligently when your date is talking. Do not interrupt. If you make comments, be sure they relate to the subject that is being discussed.

Reflect your partner's feelings—as a mirror reflects his image. Example: If your date seems pleased about something, say, "I'm glad you like it," or "You really like that, don't you?" If he or she is obviously upset, say, "I'm sorry you're upset."

Add interesting details to what is already being said. Example: If your date is talking about football, you might volunteer your early impressions of football and tell how you learned to appreciate the game.

Learn to relax during periods of silence. Neither party needs to chatter every minute during a date. Just sitting or walking together comfortably without talking can sometimes be most enjoyable.

Explain to your teen-agers that physical intimacies are neither necessary nor always expected on dates. Young, inexperienced teen-age boys get the impression from older adolescents that girls expect the boys to try to "make out" with them by kissing them, necking with them, trying to seduce them. Many young boys, shy and embarrassed because they know little about the art of pleasing a girl, avoid dating. They are afraid of girls; yet they are even more afraid of themselves and their own inadequacies.

According to the studies in adolescence, expertness at kissing, petting, and "making out" on dates is not admired by members of either sex. Make it clear to your adolescent son, therefore, that most girls neither want nor expect a boy to demonstrate his prowess as a lover. They prefer that he be polite, courteous, attentive, considerate, and respectful. In other words, they like a boy who knows how to behave himself. Such intimacies as holding hands or putting an arm about the shoulder or waist are quite harmless and are, under most circumstances, quite acceptable. But a girl's having to ward off the inept advances of a young male in wolf's clothing is another matter.

Teach your teen-agers how to end a date. Some boys and girls know when it is time to end a date, and they end it skillfully. Many others, however, seem utterly unable to take leave of each other promptly and gracefully. They linger far too long, and, although they may be bored, neither the boy nor the girl seems able to end the date.

If your teen-agers have this problem, a suggestion such as this one from you may help: "When the time comes to end a date and your partner shows no inclination to end it, say, 'Well, it's time to go now. It's been swell—I had loads of fun. Good night, John (or Henry, or Mary, or Jane). I'll see you tomorrow.' Or something like that. And that's it. Do an about-face and go into the house—or wherever you should go at the end of the date."

Settle the question of the good night kiss. What about that famous institution, the good night kiss? Strangely enough, the good night kiss is sometimes the most dreaded and, therefore, the most difficult part of the date. This attitude, which is especially prevalent among inexperienced boys, springs from feelings of inadequacy and lack of practice at demonstrating affection. The boy thinks the girl expects him to kiss her at the end of the date. Feeling insecure and afraid, he keeps putting it off, thereby prolonging the date. The girl may have to take the initiative and either present herself to be kissed or bid the boy good night and retire without being kissed.

It is probably wise to let your youngsters know how you feel about the good night kiss. Perhaps you regard it as the thing to do—a harmless, friendly gesture that means, "I think you're nice," and nothing more. On the other hand, perhaps you are convinced that a girl should be extremely selective. Or, perhaps you feel that a good-night kiss is usually in order but that there are some circumstances and conditions under which it should be avoided. Perhaps there are times when saying, with a smile, "Thank you, I had a wonderful time," is more appropriate and more meaningful than a good-night kiss. Whatever you believe, discuss this matter with your teen-agers if they seem to be concerned about it. They will appreciate your interest, for it is a problem that is important to them.

Review of major points

1. Recognize the values of dating during adolescence.
2. Let *readiness* determine when dating shall begin.
3. Recognize the symptoms of readiness for dating.
4. React wholesomely to teen-agers' requests to start dating.
5. Help teen-agers develop elementary social skills that are basic and essential to successful dating.

SUMMARY

This chapter discussed dating problems that young teen-agers face and suggested ways in which parents can help youngsters meet these problems successfully.

The next chapter will continue this discussion with special reference to questions about dating that teen-agers' parents ask and suggest answers to those questions.

Chapter 7

Parents' Questions about Dating

PARENTS ASK MANY questions about dating, several of which were discussed in the previous chapter. Here are some additional important ones: How much should parents know about teen-agers' dating plans? How much should teen-agers be expected to tell their parents about what happened on a date? What about the family car? Should dating be permitted on school nights? Should teenagers be permitted to have blind dates? What attitudes should parents take on going steady? What are the advantages and disadvantages of going steady? Are there dangers inherent in this practice? The suggestions that follow may help parents formulate realistic, practical answers to these questions.

How much should parents know about teen-agers' dating plans? Some parents insist on knowing every detail about their teen-agers' dating plans, while others ask no questions at all. Most parents want to know certain facts: where their youngsters are going; with whom they are going; how they expect to travel; when they expect to leave; what they expect to do when they get there; when the activity will be over; and when they expect to arrive home. Parents should know this much about young teenagers' plans whether they have a date or are going out dateless. Indeed, it is their responsibility to know.

This is not to say that parents must be rigid or unreasonable in their demands. Quite the contrary. They may prefer not to interfere with their youngsters' plans even when they are not very happy about them. They may not be particularly joyous, for example, about the hours the youngsters keep; yet they do not want to reduce dating to punching a time clock.

Adolescents feel more secure on a date when they have briefed their parents on their plans, for then they know exactly what the parents expect of them. They know also that if they live up to their side of the bargain, the parents will continue giving them approval and moral support.

Sharing plans with parents may provide youngsters a way out of difficult situations from which they want to escape. Mary, for example, looks at her watch at one minute to eleven o'clock and says to Joe, who is becoming too romantic for comfort: "You must take me home now, Joe. My parents are expecting me at eleven o'clock. They are very strict. If I am not there right on time, they will be furious." No self-respecting teen-ager—Joe, Henry, Peter, or Bob—wants to meet Mary's parents face-to-face when they are "furious."

How much should teen-agers tell parents about what happened on a date? Adolescents who tell their parents everything that happened on a date are rare individuals indeed. Most teen-agers tell parents as little as possible. The youngsters who "tell all" are usually somewhat immature, a bit naïve, and perhaps too dependent on their parents. They reassure the parents that they are good children because they need parental approval. Teenagers who, on the other hand, tell their parents nothing about dates may have a negative, defensive relationship with them; in other words, they do not trust their parents. The feeling is often mutual—the parents do not trust their children either.

If your youngsters tell you only enough about their dates to satisfy your curiosity, be happy about it; this pattern represents normal behavior. If they want to tell you more, they will. If they do not tell you more although you are usually their confidant, perhaps they think they are able to handle their own dating problems up to this point. Regardless of how little or much your teen-agers tell you, it is wise to show you are always interested and willing to listen.

Should parents permit teen-agers to use the family car? No person, teen-ager, or adult, who does not drive competently or who does not possess a valid driver's license should ever operate an automobile. Every teen-ager who is qualified and licensed, however, should be encouraged to drive someone's car from time to time: his own, his parents', his friends'. He needs driving practice to retain his skill.

The family car creates a complex problem that cannot be solved by permitting teen-agers to use it at will. Parents are faced continually with their own needs and the responsibility of seeing that their youngsters have adequate transportation. They cannot afford to leave either of these matters to chance. If teen-agers are too young to drive, parents must drive for them. Most adolescents who are fifteen years old or older avoid this prospect, however, because they think it makes them look like children. They prefer to walk, if necessary, or to use public transportation, or to double-date with someone who does have a car.

Teen-agers who do not have cars regard double dating with car-owners as perhaps the next best thing to having their own cars. Double dating has some advantages. It provides additional companionship, for example, and is usually inexpensive. Boys share the cost of gasoline ordinarily, thereby reducing the cost per couple.

The greatest danger in sharing a ride is that sometimes the driver, although licensed, is not competent. He may drive too fast or take foolish, needless risks. If your youngsters expect to ride in someone else's car, find out who will be driving. If you know the driver is a "wild" one, see to it that your youngsters change their plans. Risks are great enough these days even when the driver is skillful; obviously, there is nothing to gain from riding with a reckless one. Too many innocent teen-agers have been mutilated or killed while riding with an irresponsible, adolescent driver who was too busy showing off to keep the car on the road.

If your adolescents are properly licensed to drive and do not have access to another car, they should probably be permitted to use the family car when the parents do not need it. If you think otherwise, have a valid reason for refusing and be sure your teen-agers know the reason and understand it. Never refuse permission without giving a good, complete explanation.

If you permit your teen-agers to use the family car, do so with certain understandings. Insist, for example, that the car be used as agreed on beforehand. Some parents require that youngsters pay for gasoline and damages that they incur. Others insist merely that the teen-agers take good care of the car. The specific points upon which you and your adolescents agree are not as important as the fact that you *agree on something* before they take the car. They know this way what you expect of them.

One important condition for releasing the family car should be that your teen-agers will exercise good judgment and reasonable caution at all times. You cannot afford to ignore poor judgment and careless driving when other people's lives, as well as those of your youngsters, are at stake.

Finally, make it clear that the right is yours at all times to withhold the privilege of using the family car, that it is your responsibility to suspend this privilege if the youngsters are negligent, careless, use poor judgment, or in any other way fail to live up to their agreement. Above all, do not hesitate to exercise this right.

Should parents permit teen-agers to have dates on school nights? Boys and girls should not have dates at night when they must go to school the next morning. The term *date* has many varieties and shades of meaning, however, and there are necessarily important exceptions to this rule. It is quite permissible, for example, for teenagers to date for an activity that they would be attending anyhow, such as choir rehearsal, play practice, or some such routine at church or at school. Dating in these instances means merely going to something with a member of the opposite sex rather than going alone or with friends of the same sex.

Studying together is another type of school-week date. This activity is all right if it works. Some teen-agers are so distracted by the date they cannot even think about their studies, much less complete them.

It is usually wise to permit dating only when there is

no school the next day. Teen-agers should keep regular hours during the week. They need enough rest, and if they are assigned homework, they are obliged to complete it. Success in school work should be as important to adolescents as success on the job will be when they are employed. They must do their academic work well and consistently if they are to succeed, just as breadwinners must produce commendable results on the job if they are to be recognized and rewarded.

How late should teen-agers stay out on dates? The answer to this question depends on answers to other questions : How old are your teen-agers? How mature are they? Are they dependable? Can you rely on them? What is the nature of the dating activity? What are the expectations of the community? How do you feel about hours for dating?

Teen-agers who have proved themselves mature, dependable, and trustworthy may be permitted more freedom generally and later hours (if they choose) than youngsters who have not yet demonstrated these qualities.

The nature of the dating activity—that is, what the youngsters expect to do on a date—determines to a large degree how late they will stay out. A double-feature movie, for example, lasts approximately four hours. Add to this the time it takes to go to the movie and to return home, and, in most instances, add the time it takes to stop for a snack on the way home. All in all, a double-feature movie date lasts five or six hours. If the date begins at seven o'clock, it is likely to end somewhere between midnight and one o'clock. If this hour is too late by your standards, there are several alternatives: the date may begin earlier; the youngsters may see only part of the movie bill; they may not stop for a snack on the way home; they may choose some other kind of activity that consumes less time. Which one shall it be? Shall you change your standards? Might a compromise be worked out? Discuss the alternatives with your youngsters; let them help you decide.

It is wise to take into account the expectations of the

community when you consider teen-agers' dating patterns. Many communities have curfew laws, for example; however, only a few communities enforce them rigidly. They employ them usually to keep teen-age loafers, floaters, vagrants, and known delinquents off the streets.

Parents should not permit youngsters to keep late hours in public places. Teen-agers can acquire a reputation for "night-owling" that, while perhaps innocent enough in itself, does not add to their social stature in the eyes of their peers. Young people who hang around public places late at night are fair game for perverts, narcotics pushers, prostitutes, and other seedy characters who are up to no good. If teen-agers must keep late hours, let them do so in the safety of their own homes where their parents may have at least some notion about what they are doing.

The hour your teen-agers are to return home from a date should be discussed and agreed to before the youngsters leave the house, and this agreement should be honored at all costs. Parents must allow a little leeway— twenty or thirty minutes in either direction— on the time for arriving home. But they should show concern when there are gross discrepancies between promises made and promises kept, for such inconsistencies are often symptomatic of deeper disturbances in the youngsters themselves or in their relationship with the parents.

Should parents encourage teen-agers to double-date? Some parents prefer that their teen-agers go out with one or more couples—that is, double-date rather than solo-date. They believe social experience is more meaningful when it is shared with other couples, and the chances for becoming intimate are fewer when a boy and a girl are with others than when they are alone together.

Most teen-agers like to double-date, but only on certain terms. They and their associates must be companionable to enjoy being together. Furthermore, they must share common likes and dislikes; otherwise, they are likely to irritate one another. Young people who entertain wide differences in values, beliefs, and attitudes are usually better off to forget about double dating.

It is probably best to leave the matter of double dating to your youngsters' judgment as a rule. They probably know—or will soon learn from experience—whether they like it or not.

Should parents permit teen-agers to have blind dates? Teen-agers may ask parents' permission to go out occasionally with individuals whom they have never met but who are willing to date "sight unseen." This kind of dating—blind dating—causes parents considerable anxiety at times, for they never know what their youngsters are getting themselves into. They may wonder, for example, why a boy should be so hard up for a date that he would want to take out a girl whom he has never met, or why a teen-age girl who is asked to go on a blind date would accept when she has no difficulty getting regular dates.

There are circumstances that make blind dating necessary. For example, teen-agers from out of town may need a date arranged before they arrive. If these boys and girls know how to behave themselves, everything may go off very well. If not, they may be interested only in racking up as many conquests as possible during their short stay in town.

Parents should probably feel concerned and somewhat dubious about their adolescents' having blind dates. It is usually more satisfactory when youngsters meet their prospective dates before they accept. If this is not possible, parents and teen-agers should formulate criteria to guide them with reference to blind dates. Here are some suggestions you might consider.

Permit your teen-agers to go only on blind dates arranged by friends whom you know are interested in promoting their welfare, not their social demise.

Meet the blind date yourself if possible. Meeting a boy is easy, for he should call at the house for your daughter—no exceptions. Meeting a girl is often difficult and sometimes impossible.

Be sure you know where your youngsters are going and what they expect to do. The place should be reputable; the activity should be desirable. Blind dates should be entertained ordinarily at a group function (such as a church, a school, or a home). The activity should, of course, be supervised by responsible adults.

The time for getting home from a bund date should be earlier as a rule than that for arriving home from a regular date.

Should parents encourage teen-agers to go steady? The "problem" of going steady receives much attention today; yet it is by no means a new one. Teen-agers and parents have been debating the merits of going steady for at least three generations. Before that, going steady was almost synonymous with being engaged—a concept far removed from its meaning today.

Most parents question the merits of going steady during early adolescence. They think it is better to date many members of the opposite sex to gain wide social experience. They believe a youngster should not limit himself to one individual. This attitude would seem to be essentially sound.

Studies of adolescent behavior reveal that girls start going steady sooner than boys and that the boys whom they date steadily are one, two, or three years older than they. This pattern is in harmony with the girls' earlier attainment of maturity. The Gesell Institute studies reported by Ilg and Ames, which we have discussed, indicate this fact quite clearly. An earlier study by Frances Bibb at the Indiana State Teachers College throws more light on this pattern. Here are Bibb's figures, based on answers of more than one thousand high school students in grades nine through twelve:

Age of Student (in years)	Percentage of Boys Going Steady	Percentage of Girls Going Steady
14	5%	13%
15	12%	20%
16	14%	22%
17	16%	25%
18-19	25%	26%

Bibb's figures and the Ilg and Ames report do not reflect the entire picture of teen-agers' heterosexual habits in America. They make no reference, for example, to the many girls and a few boys who drop out of high school to get married. This number is quite large, as suggested by the fact that half of all the first marriages in America involve brides who are not yet twenty years old. And many more girls get married soon after they complete high school.

What are the advantages and disadvantages of going steady? Parents' and teen-agers' discussions of going steady are often very heated ones, based on emotions more than on facts. There are actually both advantages and disadvantages to going steady that you should consider objectively before you discuss the matter with your teenagers. Here are some of them:

Advantages

Going steady gives the adolescent more time with the person whom he likes best—his "one and only."

Going steady gives the youngster the security of knowing that he has a date whenever he wants one. This certainty relieves him from worry; he does not wonder whether he will be able to get a date.

Going steady gives youngsters status among peers. Teen-agers regard the person who is going steady as being more mature than others. They think the individual has "something on the ball"—otherwise, he would not rate a steady date.

Going steady gives a couple the opportunity to know each other in depth by being together in a variety of situations and seeing each other under many different circumstances. This deeper kind of relationship challenges the adolescent to accept a member of the opposite sex on a more realistic plane and to make adjustments in himself that will help him get along better in the adult heterosexual relationship.

Couples who go steady appear to be more sensible than other boys and girls their age. They go out less frequently as a rule than regular daters, and they spend less money.

They get more fun out of doing ordinary things: studying together, watching television, doing chores about the home, "just talking," "just being together," taking a walk or a ride.

The boy and girl who go steady confide in each other, thereby securing valuable release from inner tensions.

Disadvantages

Going steady is too restrictive. It causes the teen-ager to avoid—and to be avoided by—members of the opposite sex who may have more to offer than the steady date.

Going steady makes it impossible for an adolescent to get the wide range of social experiences that he must have to choose wisely for marriage. He can obtain adequate experience only through dating many different persons.

A boy and a girl who go steady spend too much time alone together. They miss the benefits that accrue ordinarily from participating in many social group activities.

Boys and girls who go steady deny themselves the opportunity to know many other adolescents at all.

Going steady is sometimes used as a means of escape by youngsters who feel insecure and inadequate in the larger group. Going steady makes it unnecessary for them to reveal their feelings to others.

Going steady ties some youngsters down too much. If the steady date is absent on vacation for several days, weeks, or months, the partner who is left behind must decide either to be "true" and dateless or be a "two-timer" and have dates. Either alternative tends to create feelings of anxiety.

Some youngsters get tired of going with one person, but they do not know how to break off the relationship without hurting the partner's feelings. Some couples continue going steady indefinitely although they are thoroughly bored.

5 Teen-agers feel sometimes that their steady date takes them for granted; yet they seldom do anything about it because they are afraid they will destroy the relationship.

Teen-agers who have been going steady for a long time and then have broken off the relationship find it difficult to get back into circulation.

Going steady may increase the likelihood that a couple will become sexually involved. Boys and girls who go steady have many more opportunities to neck and pet in private for long periods of time. This kind of activity may culminate in coitus.

As a result of "going too far too soon," some steady daters discover suddenly that they are expectant parents. Faced with the problem of deciding what to do about the pregnancy, they have certain alternatives: get an illegal abortion, have the baby out of wedlock, or get married. None of these choices really solves the problem; each choice represents only the first step toward a solution that is rarely satisfactory.

How may parents and teen-agers resolve the question of going steady? All of the arguments for going steady and those against the practice have some merit. What position, then, should parents take on this issue? Parents must decide this matter for themselves. They should decide, however, on the basis of evidence rather than emotion or prejudice.

It is probably wise to encourage younger adolescents —thirteen-, fourteen-, and fifteen-years-olds and a few immature sixteen-year-olds—to postpone going steady until they are more mature and have accumulated more social skills by dating many different individuals. Beyond sixteen, going steady is usually inevitable.

Many youngsters ask permission to go steady long before their parents think they are ready. Never make fun of younger adolescents for wanting to go steady; the social pressure for a steady date is often very strong. The problem is serious to teen-agers, and parents should treat it seriously.

If your younger adolescents want to go steady before you think they are ready, discuss with them the advantages and disadvantages outlined above. Knowing there are disadvantages as well as advantages to going steady may help them resolve the problem to your satisfaction and theirs.

Review of major points

1. Know your youngsters' dating plans in considerable detail.
2. Be interested in teen-agers' dating experiences when they want to share them with you.
3. Lend the family car to teen-agers only under well-defined rules and regulations.
4. Restrict dating generally to non-school nights.
5. Insist that your teen-agers keep reasonable hours when they date.
6. Let your youngsters decide (within reasonable limits) about double dating.
7. View blind dates with caution and concern.
8. Face realistically the question of going steady.
9. Weigh the advantages of going steady against the disadvantages.
10. Help your teen-agers resolve the question of going steady to their satisfaction and yours.

SUMMARY

This chapter posed dating questions asked by parents of teen-agers and suggested possible solutions to these problems.

The next chapter will discuss sex during adolescence and suggest ways in which parents may help youngsters build wholesome, constructive sex attitudes into their lives.

Chapter 8

Wholesome Sex Attitudes

TEEN-AGERS NEED competent, thorough, extensive sex education and guidance more desperately today than ever before in the nation's history; yet objective studies suggest they are not getting it in sufficient amounts, nor is what they get as effective as it should be.

The difficulties in resolving this problem lie in part, at least, in the changing values of our culture. Teen-agers' behavior reflects adults' freedom and looseness in heterosexual relationships, loss of respect for the traditional virtues, confusion of sex roles in the culture.

Teen-agers have always been deeply concerned about sex, but modern teen-agers are notably confused. Only a few parents, unfortunately, give them the help they need.

Drs. Lawrence K. and Mary Frank declare in *Your Adolescent at Home and in School,* "Central in young people's troubled thinking is the question of place, meaning, and use of sex—how human sexuality differs from animal mating; how males differ from females in sex interest, desire, and responsiveness. Adolescents are puzzled and anxious—and, let us be honest, so are many adults."

Most parents want genuinely to help their youngsters think clearly about sex, develop wholesome sex attitudes,, express their sexual urges in ways that are constructive. The suggestions that follow may help parents perform this task.

Take a wholesome, positive attitude toward sex in human life. Many forces in our culture make sex appear questionable, suspicious, basically undesirable. Small children are often taught, for example, never to touch their genitals, never to show them, never to talk about anything that pertains to sex. Their normal sex curiosity is often crushed by society's attitude that it is not nice to

93

think about such things. Yet sex, mildly camouflaged, ranks high in the adult culture, being perhaps the human factor used most frequently in commercial advertising, movies, theatre, magazines, and other mass media. People buy products that they think will make them more attractive to members of the opposite sex; likewise, they seek entertainment that conveys the message of love. Yet they often reject normal sexual development and expression in boys and girls.

Sex is an integral part of living; it plays a major role in human life, human happiness, continuance of the human race. Sex is not vile, dirty, or base. It becomes so only when it is misinterpreted, misdirected, misused. Parents who convey this fundamental attitude to their youngsters give them a start in the right direction.

Accept your parental responsibility to help your teenager build sex into his life. Parents are primarily responsible for helping their children develop wholesome sex attitudes and acceptable sex practices. The most important time for doing this is, of course, during the early years of life—infancy and early childhood, when the child's mind and moral sense are developing.[1] Yet the parent's job is not complete until his children are mature, able, and willing to apply sex knowledge and attitudes intelligently with an adult sense of responsibility.

If parents do their job effectively in sex education, there is little to worry about. Unfortunately, many of them admittedly do not know what to do; others do nothing at all because they are afraid of the subject. Dr. H. H. Remmers, director of the Purdue Opinion Panel, found in a nationwide survey, for example, that 20 per cent of the teen-agers said their parents consciously *avoid* discussing sex with them. Another twenty per cent of all parents are probably willing to discuss sex but do not know enough about the subject to be of much help.

[1] For delineation of this thesis, see *How To Give Your Child A Good Start in Life,* by Leland E. Glover (New York: Collier Books, 1961), Ch. 7, "Establishing Sex Identity and Developing Positive Feelings About Sex."

Parents who avoid discussing sex with their youngsters and those who are not adequately informed on the subject may do more harm than they realize. Mrs. Katheryn Nielsen, Executive Director of the Los Angeles Florence Crittenton Home, a residential institution for unwed mothers, says most pregnant girls whom she sees have been "sadly prepared" to cope with the emotional aspects of sex life. "What has shocked us most," she declares, "is the unwed teen-age mother's utter lack of knowledge of the differences between the male and female sex drives."

Teen-agers must learn more from their parents than the "facts of life." They need the right feelings, the right attitudes, the right emotions, which grant sex the splendid place in life it deserves. They get these feelings, attitudes, and emotions not from books nor from lectures, which admittedly yield useful information; rather they get them from their parents, day by day, year by year, living with them in the family.

Encourage your youngster to take sex education classes in school and at church. Parents should give their youngsters all the sex information they need, answer their questions honestly, sincerely, without embarrassment or shame. Parents, effective as they may be, still need help from the school and the church to round out their children's sex education.

Many schools offer human growth and development units with emphasis on sex and reproduction. These objective, scientific, dispassionate courses give boys and girls important information and insights.

The church teaches religious, moral, and spiritual aspects of sex in human life as well as the physical facts. If you want your teen-ager to develop sex behavior that is in harmony with his religious convictions, be sure he attends sex education classes offered in the church.

If your youngster's school and church lack such instruction, you may request that it be installed. Your best bet with the schools is to work through a curriculum committee of the Parent-Teachers Association (PTA). In the church or synagogue, discuss the matter with other parents, organize an *ad hoc* committee, and present your proposal to the minister or rabbi.

Understand and accept normal sexual drives and permissible sexual outlets for teen-agers as individuals. Sex dreams, nocturnal emissions, masturbation, and many other psycho-physiological characteristics of adolescence are quite normal and universal. Parents accept ordinarily most normal sexual patterns in adolescents; or, at least, they don't combat them. Other parents, however, do object to some normal practices because they suffer feelings of self-guilt or are perhaps merely misinformed.

Masturbation is probably the most misunderstood sexual activity in the lives of teen-agers; at the same time, it is the one that is most widely practiced. Research studies, including those of Dr. Alfred Kinsey, indicate that almost all adolescent boys masturbate to orgasm in isolation as the primary means to release from sexual tension. Girls, being less commonly aware of their sexual sensitivity potential, are not as active as boys; studies indicate that perhaps only half of them masturbate to climax before they are married. Middle- and upper-class boys masturbate as the *primary* source of sexual release until they are married. Lower-class boys, however, regard masturbation as infantile and substitute illicit sexual intercourse for it, whenever possible, soon after puberty.

Masturbation was long regarded as being self-abusive, damaging to mind and emotions, likely to lead to insanity. Such ideas as these were completely preposterous; yet they were widely disseminated at the turn of the century by a Dr. Gunn in his book, *The Family Physician,* which equated sex with sin, labeled masturbation the most degrading and self-damaging of all sins. Woe be to the child who masturbated! Dr. Gunn's ideas were accepted, unfortunately, and believed by a gullible public. Little wonder parents tried to keep their youngsters' hands off their genitals. Their efforts were in vain. Their attempts to heed Dr. Gunn's warnings simply confused their boys and girls.

Today, authorities on sex—physicians, psychologists,

psychoanalysts, church leaders, and others—agree that exploring the genitals is normal, harmless, probably helpful to small children. In fact, experts are inclined to worry about youngsters who do not do these things, since to refrain entirely is not normal.

Walter Stokes, M.D., expresses a professional view regarding self-gratification that is generally shared by other leaders in medicine and related fields: "I have arrived at the view, after a lifetime of clinical experience with sex problems, that the time has come not only to throw out all traces of our ancient negative ideas about masturbation but boldly and unequivocally to defend it and give it the important affirmative position it should have in any rational concept of personality structure and social relations."[2]

Unfortunately, most teen-agers have been taught from an early age that it is "naughty" or wrong or harmful to pay attention to their genitals. Consequently, when natural, normal sex feelings urge them to masturbate, they feel guilty and ashamed; furthermore, if they are discovered, they are usually traumatized. The important thing parents should remember is this: *The act of masturbating is harmless; the hurt comes only from feeling guilty and ashamed.* The rightful duty of the parent is to relieve the youngster's feelings of guilt and shame and reassure him that the practice is harmless, normal, universal.

Understand the common patterns of sexual behavior in teen-age dating. Dating in this section refers to dates that involve only one couple, a boy and a girl. The sexual behavior patterns of adolescent boys and girls on dates are definitely known through research studies. It is important that parents understand them so they may help their teen-agers cope with them.

Teen-agers show considerable tension and anxiety about what may be expected of them on dates; they wonder and worry about the practices they may encounter. The Purdue

[2] Stokes, Walter R., LL.B., M.D., "Modern View of Masturbation," *Sexology*, April, 1961, pp. 588-589.

Opinion Panel, reported by Dr. Remmers in *The American Teenager,* indicates that many high school students are worried about such questions as these: Should I kiss my date the first time? Must I neck to be popular? Should high school students pet and make love? How far (toward sexual intercourse) should high school students go?

The middle-class American teen-ager's pattern of sexual behavior on dates, as revealed in several studies, seems to be this: the first date may involve merely holding hands. A good-night kiss at the door after the first date is not unheard of; however, it is usually considered better to wait a while. After the second or third date, holding hands and good-night kisses are the rule. Subsequent dates find the couple necking, which consists of kissing and hugging, confining the principal activities to those areas above the shoulders. Next comes petting, which goes beyond necking to include exploring and stimulating the partner's body, especially the sensuous zones. Light petting includes only mild stimulation; heavy petting, on the other hand, includes profound stimulation and sexual excitement that may include orgasm.

Teen-agers from middle-class homes start dating usually when they are about fifteen or sixteen years old. They pet frequently, but they do not often "go all the way"; that is, they stop short of coitus, as a rule, and suppress their sexual urgencies in favor of chastity. They obtain sexual release sometimes through masturbation afterward when they are alone at home. However, a modest percentage of them do "go all the way."

Teen-agers from lower-class homes, in contrast to middle-class youngsters, start dating usually at an earlier age, when they are twelve, thirteen, or fourteen years old. They emphasize having sexual intercourse rather than petting. Boys from lower-class homes frown on petting and masturbation. Their fathers encourage them to "act like men"—that is, to have intercourse. The boys want to have intercourse without preliminary demonstration of affection and without displaying appreciation afterward. Thus, the girl becomes the object of the male's sexual aggression, not a valued, respected partner in tender love making. (This attitude reflects also the typical pattern of sexual behavior between husband and wife in lower-class marriages.)

Warn your teen-ager of the dangers involved in necking and petting. Anthropologist Dr. Margaret Mead, who abhors the emphasis on early dating in our culture, observed recently that petting became solidly established in the adolescent way of life some years ago and soon became standard practice for all teen-agers except ". . . the very timid, the very morally intimidated, and the very unattractive." Teen-agers today, with the aid of automobiles and parental guarantees of freedom, secure petting privacy on secluded streets, in drive-in theatres, and elsewhere. This is a "fact of life" parents must face.

Parents who fail to warn their youngsters in realistic terms of the dangers of petting do them a great disservice. Parents should not try to frighten teen-agers out of their wits; rather, they should merely tell them the facts, the possibilities, the things to keep in mind. These data, when carefully considered and thoughtfully absorbed, are often sufficient to keep teen-agers out of trouble.

Holding hands, kissing, hugging, and similar teenage demonstrations of friendship and affection are, as a rule, quite harmless in themselves; however, the goal to which they are likely to lead may be harmful, perhaps disastrous. Light petting is essentially what many happily married couples do in private to express affection in a playful manner. Heavy petting, however is the logical preliminary to sexual intercourse. This phase of love making, termed foreplay, is highly recommended in marriage because it prepares the female fully for intromission and rapid attainment of climax. Many teen-age girls who intend to remain chaste lose control unwittingly in the heat of passion and "go all the way" with the boy, only to regret later having done so. They would not have submitted to intercourse had they not started petting in the first place.

Dr. Evelyn Duvall, in *Facts of Life and Love for Teen-Agers,* advises girls to learn the symptoms a boy displays when, as a result of petting, he is about to get out of hand. She advises the girl to stop everything at this point, explain to the boy that it is time to quit. The symptoms she describes in the boy (face flushed, rapid breathing, etc.) are typically those of the human male immediately prior to intromission, which commences intercourse. Unfortunately, the boy at this point is usually in no condition to stop, nor is the girl likely to stop him if she is equally excited. Dr. Duvall does recognize the dangers of unplanned coitus as a result of heavy petting and warns the girl against it.

Studies of teen-age dating behavior indicate clearly that most middle-class boys expect the girl to set limits regarding petting; then they test the limits, urge her to go farther, but do not demand it. Thus, the middle-class girl who pets but avoids intercourse does so because *she* chooses this pattern, not because it is necessarily the boy's choice too. Parents are wise, therefore, who warn their daughters not to lead boys on nor to permit them to go as far as they might suggest. The girl who permits a boy to pet with her to the brink of coitus invites trouble; furthermore, she is being quite unfair to the boy if she permits him to go that far when she is determined to avoid coitus.

The intelligent, informed, levelheaded parent does not recommend that his daughter indulge in sexual intercourse prior to marriage. Teen-age girls are wise who keep their minds clear and exercise good judgment at all times when they are out on dates. And parents are wise who tell them they should do just that—and then explain why.

Sexual intercourse, the logical goal of heavy petting, involves the risk of pregnancy out of wedlock, an occurrence that is all too common in modern America. The National Office of Vital Statistics, an agency of the federal government, announced in 1960 that the rate of motherhood out of wedlock is steadily increasing and that most of this increase is in the teen-age population. This trend may be observed in homes for unwed mothers, where girls are most frequently about seventeen years old when the baby arrives—which means they conceived when they were sixteen years old. The age range is wide, however. The director of a home told me recently the youngest unwed mother whom she interviewed was only twelve years old, the oldest was forty-eight.

An alternative to motherhood out of wedlock is a quick, hurried-up marriage to legitimatize the baby. Many pregnant teen-age girls do get married, have the baby, then secure a divorce. In doing so, they lower the nation's average age for initial marriage, the average age for first birth in wedlock, the average age for initial divorce.

Illegal abortion is another alternative to unwed motherhood. This course of action is often selected by middle-class persons, if studies of the practice may be regarded as valid. Baltimore's G. Lotrell Timanus, M.D., the most famous medical abortionist of all time, kept careful records of his practice from 1920 to 1951, during which time he performed 5,210 illegal operations. Approximately three per cent of his patients were twelve to fifteen years old, almost 14 per cent were sixteen to twenty years old. Thus, approximately 17 per cent of the abortions he performed involved girls who were too young to vote. Almost none of these girls were married; almost all of them were brought or sent to the abortionist by their parents.[8] These figures are probably fairly representative of other abortionists' figures, very few of which are recorded or made known to the public. Dr. Timanus, a competent, highly regarded physician with a heavy illicit case load (he maintained a roster of 353 physicians who referred abortion cases to him, including, in some instances, their own wives and daughters), said he only lost four patients during thirty-one years' practice—*a.* remarkable medical record.

[8]Dr. Timanus's courtroom testimony appears in *Abortion in the United States* (New York: Harper-Hoeber, 1958), the record of the 1955 International Conference on Abortion sponsored by the Planned Parenthood Federation of America and the New York Academy of Medicine.

He had the best medical facilities available and fully trained assistants. Most abortionists, however, are ill-trained, poorly equipped; many of them are not even doctors. Consequently, the girl who goes to an abortionist to solve her premarital pregnancy problem risks her own mental and emotional stability—and her very life. Most physicians recommend motherhood without marriage as being preferable to criminal abortion.

These are some of the facts of life you should discuss with your teen-agers. It is not enough to tell them, as did one mother of a teen-ager who later got pregnant out of wedlock: "Stay out of trouble!" Most teen-agers know very little about how to get in trouble or how to stay out of it. It is the parent's responsibility to tell youngsters the dangers of sexual intimacies *before* they have the opportunity to take chances, not after they have taken them and gotten trapped.

Explain the fallacy of testing "sexual compatibility'* *before marriage.* Studies by Dr. Winston Ehrmann, Dr. Lester Kirkendall, and other researchers indicate that most middle-class teen-age girls who participate in coitus prior to marriage do so to please a boyfriend or to try to cement an affectional relationship with him. Unfortunately (from the girl's point of view, at least), submitting sexually to a boyfriend may signal the end of the romance, especially when it occurs early in courtship. Such a coital experience takes place usually under circumstances that fall far short of ideal for sexual fulfillment—hasty, hurried up, fearful love-making in the back seat of a car, for example, on a lonely street, perhaps, with additional fears of being caught. There are usually additional fears about self— feelings of guilt for breaking society's laws, fears of conceiving, fears of contracting venereal disease. Such elements as these preclude the possibility of testing accurately a couple's sexual compatibility. Even in normal marriage, where all conditions are in the partners' favor, sexual relations that gratify both partners may often take weeks, months, even years of practice to develop fully. It is ridiculous to expect to learn anything important, therefore, by such "tests" by teen-agers out of wedlock.

It is your responsibility to convey this message to your teen-agers.

Warn your youngsters about venereal disease. Gonorrhea and syphilis, the major venereal diseases, were generally feared and abhorred until certain miracle drugs, principally penicillin, were found to be effective when administered early in the illness. Unfortunately, caution and good sense regarding venereal disease have given way to carelessness and overconfidence; as a result, the incidence of venereal infection is today the highest in the nation's history, and it is still growing. The United States Public Health Service describes the trend as ". . . shocking—a serious threat to our nation's health and security." The rise in the venereal disease rate throughout the nation is almost too great for one to comprehend. Here are some examples: New Orleans—818 per cent increase in reported cases of syphilis in the four years, 1955 to 1959. Los Angeles and San Francisco—200 per cent increase in reported cases of syphilis in two years, 1959 to 1960. Two million untreated cases of syphilis are at large in the nation; 60,000 new cases are contracted each year. Six million cases of untreated gonorrhea are at large; 2,000,000 new cases are contracted each year. *More than 20 per cent of all new cases of syphilis and gonorrhea reported are teen-agers, almost none of whom are married.* The U. S. Public Health Service declares, "The rise in venereal disease rates is absolute in every category across the country—male and female, poor and rich, young and old, colored and white, urban and rural." The only relatively sure way teen-agers may avoid venereal infection is to avoid sexual relations. Almost all cases of new infection, according to health authorities, are directly traceable to contact with the genitals of an infected person, usually during sexual intercourse. "Nice" boys and girls from middle- and upper-class homes are not exempt; they are just as susceptible to infection as youngsters from lower-class homes and poverty-stricken neighborhoods. A study by health officials of a venereal disease epidemic in a California junior college, for example, revealed that almost all of the girls were infected *by their steady boyfriends!* The boys had strayed, contracted the disease from a promiscuous girl or a prostitute, and had then infected the steady girlfriend before they knew they were ill.

The Public Health Service urges parents, teachers, church leaders to educate young people regarding venereal disease, to warn them of its dangers, and, above all, to urge them to get medical treatment *at once* if they ever contract a disease. New cases can usually be cured rather quickly if they are treated early. If, on the other hand, there is too long a delay, a cure is much more difficult, and, in some instances, is no longer possible.

Realize that there is no additional safety in numbers among teen-agers. The popular belief exists that couples who date singly are more likely to become sexually involved than do those who date as members of a group. This belief is probably erroneous. Studies suggest that many youngsters who, as individuals, are quite well-behaved, take on unwholesome behaviors of the group to which they belong. For example, someone in Johnny's group displays a bottle of whiskey, takes a drink, passes the bottle around. Johnny, who would not drink under ordinary circumstances, takes a swallow or two to be "one of the gang." This pattern may also include smoking, necking and petting, coitus, experimenting with marijuana and narcotics—all because "everybody's doing it."

Some parents, well-meaning but naïve, have returned home to find the house filled to overflowing with their teen-ager's friends in various states of undress, compromising positions, intoxicated with liquor and sexual excitement. They have waded through debris that included empty bottles, misplaced furniture, torn up carpets. They have discovered to their dismay that the kids, who insisted they were "just having a little fun," deeply resented the intrusion! A group of forty-five youngsters in a well-to-do Chicago suburb were recently found to be steady participants in sex parties that took place, for the most part, in their own parents' home during the parents' absence. This pattern has been repeated periodically in teen-age groups across the nation.

Parents should know where their teen-agers are at all times and whom they are with. They should never permit them use of the house without competent, adequate adult supervision. To do so is to court disaster.

Nor is there necessarily safety in numbers in single-sex groups. Several studies, including those by Dr. Alfred Kinsey, Dr. Winston Ehrmann, and Dr. Lester Kirkendall, indicate, for example, that teen-age boys who visit prostitutes do so usually as members of a male group. None of them would be likely to go alone. They "go along with the gang" to reassure themselves of their own masculinity, and to gain status with their male friends by "proving themselves" with a prostitute. These boys are usually older teen-agers.

Girls, too, may do things as members of a group that they would not do alone. Arthur J. Rogers, Assistant to the Commissioner of Youth Services in New York, says groups of girls affiliated with delinquent gangs of boys ". . . will do anything to please members of gangs they are affiliated with. . . . They are promiscuous, truant, violent. They participate in petty theft, have out-of-wedlock pregnancies, use alcohol and narcotics excessively."

Most boys and girls do not behave in these ways; for this fact we parents are grateful. But these shocking examples are given here to illustrate the fact that the group may influence profoundly the behavior of the individual. Parents must be sure, therefore, that their teenager associates with constellations of youngsters who are clean, wholesome, constructive in their sex attitudes and activities. They must encourage him to avoid friendships with groups of youngsters who are likely to influence him in the wrong direction.

Warn your youngsters about the ways alcohol and marijuana influence sexual behavior. Teen-agers should know that liquor lowers the individual's inhibitions, beclouds his good judgment, lets him do things he would never do if he were not under the influence of alcohol. Thus, the teen-age girl is much more likely to "go all the way" with a boy when she has had a drink or two—or three.

Marijuana acts like alcohol in some ways; however, it is more powerful, lasts longer, and is more likely to result in sexual orgies.

Parents hope, of course, that their teen-agers will stay away from liquor and marijuana. They expect them to do so. However, modern teen-agers have easy access to liquor, and they can get marijuana without trying too hard. Many of them are tempted to try them out "just to see how it feels." Parents should think realistically, therefore, about these vices, warn their youngsters against them. They must not ignore the problem nor wait passively, hoping their teen-agers will have the good sense not to experiment when urged by others to do so.

Warn your teen-agers against "pick-up" contacts, clandestine meetings, dating persons with "bad" reputations. Everything that has been mentioned thus far that implies *danger* in teen-age sexual behavior—pregnancy out of wedlock, venereal disease, influence of unwholesome groups, liquor, marijuana—applies doubly to pick-up contacts, clandestine meetings, and dating persons who have earned reputations for sexual aggressiveness, sexual submissiveness, or some other form of asocial sexual behavior.

Teen-age boys, especially those in small groups, try sometimes to pick up teen-age girls, take them riding in cars, take liberties with their bodies, have sexual intercourse with them if they can. Teen-age girls, flattered by the attention they receive while walking alone or in pairs, may encourage boys by smiling, laughing, urging them on. Sometimes they get in the car with them—in which case, they are asking for trouble.

Parents should inform boys that girls who permit themselves to be picked up on the street are the ones most likely to cause them trouble in many ways: accuse them of rape, give them venereal disease, help them establish a "bad" reputation. Parents should warn their teen-age daughter against permitting herself to be picked up. The consequences of being picked up may be rape, venereal disease, "bad" reputation, violence, death.

Clandestine meetings with members of either sex are as dangerous, in most instances, as are pick-up contacts. The girl who meets a boy in secret does not know what is in store for her, especially when she does not know him very well. If she meets a girl under these circumstances, she is vulnerable to that girl's whims, be they wholesome or deviate. Again, *parents should know where their teenagers are at all times.* There should be no room in youngsters' lives for a secret rendezvous about which their parents are ignorant.

Dating a person with an established reputation for promiscuous sexual behavior is, of course, asking for trouble. It implies, in the first place, that the innocent teen-ager approves promiscuous behavior; secondly, it implies that he himself probably expects to become promiscuous. Perhaps the innocent teen-ager neither accepts sexual promiscuity nor expects to share in it; nevertheless, this is not the impression he creates. He is likely, therefore, to share that person's reputation in any case. And, of course, if he imitates the behavior, that is even worse. The only reasonable course is, therefore, to avoid associating with this individual.

Parents sometimes must exercise maximum authority to prevent unwholesome alliances, and should do so without question, without hesitation, without apology.

Inform your youngsters about sexual deviates. Deviations from normal sexual behavior are not pleasant subjects for discussion; nonetheless, teen-agers should know about them. The most common one is homosexuality, which involves sexual attraction and possibly sexual contact between two members of the same sex.

Homosexual feelings among teen-agers are rather common, especially during early adolescence, when girls get crushes on girls and boys still prefer boys as companions. However, such feelings are usually transitory; they disappear normally as youngsters become more mature and turn their attentions to members of the opposite sex. The danger is present, nevertheless, from confirmed homosexuals of each sex who seek teen-age boys or girls as companions, try to seduce them and convert them to a homosexual way of life. Parents should tell their youngsters about homosexuals, warn them to be on guard.

Other deviates about whom teen-agers should know include sexual *sadists* (who derive pleasure from being cruel to the partner); *voyeurs* (who derive pleasure from "peeping" at girls); *molesters* (who enjoy disrobing and molesting boys and/or girls, especially young children); *rapists* (who derive pleasure from forcing a female to participate in the sex act); *transvestites* (who derive pleasure from dressing as members of the opposite sex); *exhibitionists* (who derive pleasure from exhibiting their genitals); *sexual psychopaths* (who may commit horrible sexual crimes without feeling guilty for having committed them). Many more patterns exist, too many to describe here. The important point is this: teen-agers should know that people such as these exist so that they may protect themselves if necessary. Parents should secure authoritative information—from the public library, for example— for their children's welfare and their own.

Listen to your teen-ager; answer his questions honestly. Teen-agers ask parents a legitimate question, expect a reasonable, helpful answer, but are sometimes turned away instead with the attitude that "nice" people don't discuss such matters. Teen-agers find this experience most frustrating. They need parents who will listen patiently to their problems and who will help, to the best of their ability, to find sound solutions.

Helping a youngster involves giving him answers. Sometimes it means directing him to people or places where he may find the right answers himself. Sometimes the parent can do no more, should do no more, than listen, listen, listen as the teen-ager verbalizes his confusions, clears his own path through the forest of adolescent doubts and fears. The adolescent needs his parent as his dependable, durable listening post. Sympathetic listening always helps a teen-ager grow up.

Retain your teen-ager's confidence at any cost. Loss of confidence in a parent is a damaging development to any teen-ager; in fact, it may cause him to reverse his normally exemplary behavior, slide quickly into a delinquent pattern.

Studies of counseling outlets indicate that most teen-agers still regard one parent—usually Mother—as the most important confidant in their lives, even when they appear to be in full revolt against parental authority and utterly devoted to their peers. Girlfriends and boyfriends also are important—more important in many households than Father, since the man of the house is usually absent all day.

Parents should expect their teen-agers to depend less on them for direct advice than they did as preadolescents; furthermore, they should accept gracefully this adjusted role. They should, above all, leave ways open to communication so that their youngsters may come to them whenever they need them.

The dangers and risks that are typically present in teenage heterosexual dating have been presented sharply in this discussion to make parents doubly aware of them. Your personal relationship as a confidant with your teen-ager should be so secure that, should he encounter any such dangers or fall victim to them, he may come without hesitation to you for sympathetic understanding, helpful counseling and sound advice.

Review of major points

1. Take a wholesome, positive attitude toward sex in human life.
2. Accept your parental responsibility to help your teen-ager bund sex constructively into his life.

3. Encourage your youngster to take sex education classes in school and at church.
4. Understand and accept normal sexual drives and permissible sexual outlets for teen-agers as individuals.
5. Understand the common patterns of sexual behavior in teen-age solo dating.
6. Warn your teen-ager of the dangers involved in petting.
7. Explain to your youngster the fallacy of testing "sexual compatibility" before marriage.
8. Warn your teen-agers about venereal diseases.
9. Realize that there is no additional safety in numbers in teen-age sexual behavior.

10. Warn your youngster about the ways alcohol and marijuana influence sexual behavior.
11. Warn your teen-agers against "pick-up" contacts, clandestine meetings, dating persons with "bad" reputations.
12. Inform your youngster about sexual deviates.
13. Listen to your teen-ager; answer honestly his questions about sex.
14. Retain your teen-ager's confidence—at any cost.

SUMMARY

This chapter discussed the sex factor in teen-age development and suggested ways in which parents can help their teen-ager acquire wholesome sex attitudes.

The next chapter will discuss automobiles in the lives of teen-agers and suggest ways in which parents can help their youngsters learn to drive safely and make good use of cars.

Chapter 9

Teen-agers and Automobiles

THE AUTOMOBILE HAS become an integral part of American life. To some teen-agers, the word car means simply a method of transportation. To others, however, the car represents a way to personal freedom. The teen-ager who is completely devoted to his car spends hours in it each day. He eats in it at drive-in restaurants. He watches drive-in movies from it. He parks with his girlfriend in it on lonely roads at night. His car gives him privacy of sort: It is his home away from home.

But cars can be dangerous as well as fun. The automobile is the third-ranking cause of death in America; as a killer, it follows only heart disease and cancer. Among older teen-agers and young adults under twenty-five, however, the automobile is Killer Number One: it takes the lives of more young people than any disease or any other instrument of death.

More than six million American teen-agers drive cars each year; more than two million of them are involved in accidents. Thousands of them are killed, hundreds of thousands are injured. Some of them are hurt so badly they will never be the same again.

Parents understandably ask: "What shall we do about teen-agers and cars?" The following suggestions may help parents find the best answer.

Recognize the important role of the automobile in the United States. A foreign observer says, "The American people live on wheels." The statement is true when Americans are compared with people of other nations. Nowhere else on earth are automobiles so plentiful as they are in the United States, so essential to the daily life, work, and play of the people. No other nation's economy is so dependent upon its automobile industry as is that of the United States, where one-sixth of the average family's income goes for buying cars, operating them, maintaining them.

A generation or two ago, the family car was often a luxury more than a necessity. Most houses were built with a single garage. Today a second car, which belongs to the housewife, rests beside the family car in an over-size two-car garage. The two-car family is becoming the rule, not the exception, in modern America. Now, however, two cars are often not enough. Junior comes into his own as a teen-ager; he thinks he needs a car. Thus, the nation is beginning to move to the *two-car plus* stage in which the teen-ager drives his own car, maintains it, may pay for it himself—although the parent is the legal owner, or responsible party, just as he is for the family's first and second cars.

Parents are wise who recognize the inevitability of the automobile's domination of the national scene at least during the next few decades. Inevitable, too, is the fact that most teen-agers will want to learn to drive a car.

Two million new teen-age drivers enter the streets and highways each year. They get their first licenses as full-fledged drivers when they are fourteen to eighteen years old, depending on the laws of the state in which they live: the average age for new licensees is sixteen years; most newly licensed drivers are that age.

The parent's role is to help his teen-ager become a competent, sensible, safe driver who is not likely to have an accident—to hurt himself or someone else.

Encourage your teen-ager to take behind-the-wheel driver training. Most secondary schools require that all students take a course in driver education, usually in the ninth grade, to equip them with basic information about automobiles and to develop proper attitudes toward driving. This course includes such material as proper attitudes; road courtesy; traffic laws; natural laws of friction, centrifugal force, and gravity as they apply to automobiles; physical limitations and personality traits of drivers; construction, operation and maintenance of the automobile;

driving problems commonly encountered on city streets, highways and freeways. Driver education courses are very valuable, and represent the only general instruction most young drivers get. This type of instruction is not enough, however, to insure competence as a driver. This objective requires behind-the-wheel driver training.

Driver training, which gives the learner actual behind-the-wheel experience with expert instructors, began in the mid-1930's when a single course was offered at State College, Pennsylvania. The value of the training was readily apparent; the course was soon copied across the nation. Today, approximately 60 per cent of the high schools in the United States offer driver training; more than half a million youngsters take the training each year.

Driver training pays off in better driving and fewer accidents, as indicated in findings of independent investigations. Drivers who complete the course have only one-third as many accidents as drivers who do not take it. Drivers who complete the course get only half as many citations for traffic violations as those who don't take the training. Insurance companies give reduced insurance rates as a rule to youngsters who complete behind-the-wheel training in high school because it makes them preferred risks.

The two weaknesses of driver training, when one considers the national interest, are these: it is not offered in *all* secondary schools of the nation, and it is an elective course in most states, not required of all students.

Unfortunately, approximately half of all American high school students are denied the opportunity to elect driver training by the fact that the school does not offer it. It is apparent that every secondary school in America should provide behind-the-wheel driver training.

Unfortunate, too, is the fact that in most states driver training may be taken or not as the student himself decides. The result: only about 35 per cent of the students eligible to take the driver training that is available to them actually do so; 65 per cent of them choose to go onto the streets and highways without training. In most schools where driver training is an elective subject, it is given on the student's time (before school, after school, Saturdays), and it carries no credit toward graduation. As a rule, it operates on an inadequate budget.

Driver training is most successful and most popular in the few states that *require* that a youngster complete it successfully to qualify for a driver's license. In these states, the training is given during school hours and is paid for out of tax money for general instruction.

Driver training is not expensive, especially in view of its benefits. Free to students, it cost schools approximately thirty-five dollars per trainee in 1960, according to the Association of Casualty and Surety Companies. The reduction of the incidence of accidents by 60 per cent through such training justifies manyfold the small expenditure. In addition, discounts on 1960-level insurance rates granted the graduate of driver training will save him from $177 to $298 before he reaches his twenty-fifth birthday. Thus, the training pays off handsomely financially as well as in preservation of life and limb.

Economy-minded civic groups have recently scrutinized critically many courses that they believed unnecessary, unwarranted or "frilly" offerings in the public schools. Many of these courses are among the most important subjects in the curriculum. One of them is driver training. With due respect to well-intentioned but ill-informed critics, driver training is not a frill at all; on the contrary, it is a *must* in modern America.

The automobile is sometimes a vicious killer in the hands of an untrained driver. The *Journal of the American Medical Association* supports this opinion in these words: "Too many leading educators, through ignorance, misinformation, or inertia, consider driver training a frill and would like to see it dropped. Evidence shows that youths trained in driving education programs while in high school have 40 to 66 per cent fewer violations and accidents than similar groups not so trained." The AMA asks for *more* driver training in our schools, not less. It would like to see *all* youngsters so trained before they go out onto the streets and highways as full-fledged drivers. As of 1962, only one youngster in six was so trained.

If your teen-ager's high school does not offer driver training, you will do him and other youngsters a favor by encouraging the school to offer it. If, in the meantime, your teen-ager must be taught to drive, it may be a good investment to have him take driving lessons from a competent instructor in a reputable commercial driving school. There are good driving schools and poor ones. It is your responsibility to investigate them and select a good one. Insurance companies do not give reduced rates to young men who have been trained by commercial driving schools because they have not yet determined these schools' degree of effectiveness.

The parent himself is generally the last choice as a youngster's driving instructor. Admittedly a good driver, the parent is usually emotionally involved with the teen-ager, tends to be impatient, critical, subjective. Nevertheless, the parent must often do the job himself because there is no one else to do it.

Appreciate the hazards that automobiles pose to young people. The American Medical Association is acutely aware of the murder, mayhem, and massacre that the automobile commits in gigantic proportions year by year. The American doctor spends much of his time patching up its unfortunate victims, rehabilitating those who are seriously damaged, shipping to the morgue the mutilated remains of those fatally injured. He sees daily the results of America's great adventure on wheels.

Parents of teen-agers who drive should examine carefully the facts about automobile casualties in America. In 1959, for example, almost 38,000 men, women, and children were killed by cars; 1,500,000 more were injured, 20 per cent of them (300,000) permanently injured. Almost one-fourth (8,600) of the persons killed by cars were young men and women from fifteen to twenty-five years old. Almost 13,000 of the drivers in these fatal cases were young people between fifteen and twenty-five years old. Today, one of every three teen-age drivers is involved in an accident during any twelve-months period. Teenage drivers have, proportionately, almost twice as many accidents as other drivers, and the damage they incur is usually more severe. Every eighth person involved in a fatal automobile accident is a teen-ager.

In view of these figures, it is little wonder the AMA wants to expand high school driver training programs! It is little wonder, too, that male drivers in the fifteen to twenty-five age-group pay almost double the normal automobile insurance premiums.

Understand the teen-ager's desire to drive and own a car. Most teen-agers learn to drive the family car under a parent's tutelage (although, as already mentioned, driver training in school would be more effective). They get a learner's permit, with their parent's consent, while they are being taught. With this permit, they may drive the car only when a licensed adult driver sits beside them.

The teen-ager gets his driver's license usually when he is sixteen years old. He urges his parents from then on to grant him unlimited use of the family car. It is virtually impossible to grant this request. The parents may, therefore, consider doing what the youngster has been thinking about all the time—buy him an inexpensive car of his own.

Owning a car is a prime passion of many teen-agers, some of whom look upon the automobile as a symbol of maturity, an instrument of freedom, a pathway to status among their peers. Teen-agers want to look grown-up; the car is a grown-up symbol. Car ownership implies these attributes: status, power, sociability, conformity, acceptance. Taking words from the mouths of teen-agers themselves, owning a car implies:

Status: "Johnny belongs. Johnny's got a car. Man! Look at ol' Johnny's wheels!"

Power: "All the guys like to go with Johnny. Johnny can get any girl he wants; he's got the greatest chariot."

Sociability: "Johnny's a great guy. He lets everyone

pile into his car." "I like having dates with Johnny. He's got a nice car, but he isn't stuck up about it."

Conformity: "Everybody wants a car. Johnny's lucky; he's got the greatest."

Acceptance: Johnny says to himself, "I own a car. Now the other guys will like me."

These attributes may be illusory. Johnny may or may not deserve the attention he receives—or *thinks* he receives—by owning a car. One thing is sure: if Johnny uses his car as it should be used, he will behave in a grown-up manner and deserve the grown-up symbol he drives.

Appreciate the emotional factors in teen-age driving. Adolescence is a period marked with emotional instability; remember this fact whenever you consider your teen-ager's request for a car. Emotional maturity— or lack of it— varies greatly among individuals. Some teen-agers are very immature, while others are more stable than many adults, in spite of the difficult problems they face. Girls are generally more mature than boys, emotionally as well as physically.[1] This difference is reflected in the fact that four boys are referred for psychological study in school for every girl who is referred. It is reflected also in the driving records of teen-agers. Male drivers' rates of accidents and traffic citations are much higher in proportion to their numbers than those of female drivers. This difference is reflected in the insurance rates for drivers fifteen to twenty-five years old. Male drivers' rates are about double those of female drivers, whose premiums are the same as those of persons twenty-five years old and older.

There are, of course, good drivers and poor ones of each sex. Driving a car means different things to different boys and girls. Psychologically, it serves as a projective technique; that is, the youngster tends to act out his inner

---

[1] Maturation differences between pubescent boys and girls: see pages 20-21.

feelings whenever he gets behind the wheel of a car. The well-adjusted, emotionally secure boy drives carefully, intelligently, at a safe speed, maneuvering in traffic with due regard for other people's safety as well as his own. The maladjusted, emotionally unstable youngster, on the other hand, may be afraid to drive at all, or he may become a fire-snorting demon behind the wheel, racing at breakneck speed through traffic with utter disregard for his own safety or that of anyone else.

The teen-ager who doubts deeply his own masculinity, who feels he must do something unusual, outstanding or daring to prove himself, may show off, drive too fast or take many risks. He gambles his own life and endangers the lives of others. Everyone who lives in Suburbia knows this boy. He is the one whom you hear taking off a couple of blocks away in a quiet, residential neighborhood. He guns the motor, his tires scream, skid wildly; the atmosphere shudders. Around the corner he comes on two wheels, settles down onto four as the car straightens out, roars down the street toward you as if it were the home stretch at the speedway. Zoom! There he goes. Another screeching of tires tells you he has applied the brakes. The car swerves, the tires squeal. Around the corner he goes onto the next straightaway and roars off into the distance. Mothers of small children shudder when they hear this boy's car. They are afraid that some day a child will get in this young man's way and will not be seen until it is too late. All too often, that is exactly what happens.

Dr. James Malfetti of Columbia University offers a clue to understanding what the automobile means to the teenage driver. He found that to teen-age nonviolators, "car" means simply a method of transportation; to teen-age violators, however, "car" means such things as freedom, weapon, power, love. The habitual violator feels angry, resentful, belittled; he vents his feelings on streets and highways by speeding, passing everyone, cutting in and out in an aggressive manner. He is impolite, discourteous, contemptuous. He shouts insults to other drivers.

Dr. Arnold R. Friesen, psychiatrist, and Dr. Purcell Schube, psychoanalyst, declare in the *Journal of California Medicine* that teen-agers and adults alike may use the automobile as "a convenient weapon to kill, maim, mutilate, destroy, eliminate, to declare war on the enemy." Personality flaws in drivers cause more crashes than faulty cars, poor law enforcement, traffic congestion, or physical defects in drivers. Some people—the overly aggressive, hostile, homicidal, and suicidal ones—should never be permitted to drive. This rule would apply doubly to teen-agers because their records are doubly bad. No youngster would be permitted to drive at all until he is eighteen years old because he is probably not emotionally mature enough to drive before that age.[2] •An automobile in the hands of an immature, emotionally disturbed individual, Drs. Friesen and Schube declare, ". . . is as much a weapon as a gun or a club."

Another psychiatrist, Dr. John Donnelly, Medical Director of the Institute for Living, says bluntly, "Hostile and impulsive mental attitudes are major causes of injuries and deaths from automobiles." He points out that five per cent of the drivers of the nation have more than thirty per cent of the accidents. He is convinced that these drivers use streets and highways as stages on which to act out their conflicts with humanity, especially their inner quarrels with authority. "The accident-prone driver," he declares, "rebels against authority."

The adolescent who rejects authority may try to outwit the police or outrun them as a lark, disregarding the welfare of the community. Recently, for example, police car patrolmen in a suburban community heard a collision nearby, hurried to the scene. A late-model car had been struck in the rear, and another car was fleeing the scene. The police gave pursuit. The chase continued twelve miles through business and residential areas of neighboring communities at speeds up to 100 miles an hour. The fleeing automobile went through thirteen stop signs, seven

[2] In California, where Drs. Friesen and Schube practice, sixteen-year-olds may be licensed to drive.

red lights, crossed the double line (illegally) three times. Finally, it spun out of control. The police—by this time there were twelve police cars involved—surrounded the wrecked car. They approached it on foot, revolvers drawn, prepared to shoot it out if necessary. Out of the car crawled two fifteen-year-old boys, unlicensed, too young to drive, grinning sheepishly, amused at their antics, disappointed only that they had lost the race. Miraculously, no one was hurt. The boys were cited for reckless driving and evading arrest and were turned over to the custody of their parents.

Parents are foolhardy who lend the family car carelessly to a teen-ager or thoughtlessly give him a car of his own even when he is legally old enough to drive and possesses a valid license. They must first evaluate his emotional stability as well as other qualifications to drive before they hand him the keys and wave good-bye.

Help your youngster view cars in proper perspective. The main purpose of a car is—or should be—to get its occupants from Place A to Place B and back again to Place A. It should do this task safely, efficiently, comfortably. The main purpose is *not* to get from here to there and back again faster, louder, more dramatically than anyone else, nor to get the occupants maimed or killed, nor to kill or maim others along the way. The levelheaded teen-ager sees cars as they really are. He knows that owning a car is not nearly as important as having good manners, a good reputation, a pleasing personality. His own good sense and practical judgment make more favorable impressions on teen-agers and adults alike than does his owning a car. Being sensible, he does not try to "keep up with the Jones boy," who is inalterably devoted to his "wheels."

Perhaps your teen-ager needs a car. Maybe he lives in an area where a car is necessary. In Southern California, for instance, teen-agers use cars often because distances are great and public transportation is inadequate. An unusually large proportion of teen-agers in this area drive their own cars. Under these circumstances, most young drivers are levelheaded because they use cars generally to transport the occupants efficiently, safely, comfortably.

If your teen-ager does not really need a car, I think you would be wise to withhold consent until he is older, more mature, and genuinely needs a car. He should be able to manage one then and take care of it and himself in a responsible manner.

Reconcile school, jobs, and driving. Controversy rages among parents and educators regarding the effect of teenagers' driving patterns on their academic performance in school. Many articles have appeared under well-publicized names (including movie stars and television personalities) that assert teen-agers who own cars doom themselves to failure in school and flirt with delinquency. Most of these pronouncements are based on inadequate data; the warnings are ill-advised. They tell only the negative side of the story. They have moved some school authorities, nevertheless, to banish cars from the high school campus, caused some parents to deny teen-agers use of the family car, much less permit them to have one of their own.

The twentieth century is famous for criticizing teen-agers severely, for publicizing the dramatic, sensational, undesirable aspects of their behavior. It behooves the intelligent parent, therefore, to know the facts about teen-agers' school performance as it relates to automobiles.

The oft-quoted study at Rexburg, Idaho, an atypical American small town, found that none of the A seniors drove a car; 15 per cent of the B students drove a car, as did 41 per cents of the C students, 71 per cent of the D students, 83 per cent of the F students. This dramatically depressing picture of adolescents and automobiles would lead the casual observer, who never looks beneath the surface for deeper meanings, to conclude that cars and low grades necessarily go hand in hand. This conclusion, widely publicized as fact rather than as an hypothesis, is inaccurate, unwarranted, misleading.

Unbiased surveys reveal no definite pattern or positive relationship between cars and grades. A survey was made at Artesia, New Mexico, for example, with the following findings: 27 per cent of the A students drove cars, as did 20 per cent of the B students, 23 per cent of the C students, 21 per cent of the D students, and 23 per cent of the F students. Thus, there was no significant relationship at all in Artesia between grades and driving.

At El Monte, California, Dr. Gunnar Wahlquist and Lorraine Anderson surveyed almost 1500 students in the high school. They found no significant relationship between owning a car and patterns of success or failure in school: 28 per cent of the A students owned and drove cars; so did 29 per cent of the D students. Dr. Wahlquist, on the basis of this study, believes that "... while cars often are blamed for low grades, they are more often merely a symptom of lack of school success of students who make poor grades. If a boy cannot succeed in the classroom, he may feel he can succeed by fixing up his car with a lot of chrome, lowering it, and doing the other things he thinks will make it stand out."

Other surveys support those of Artesia and El Monte; none of them support the Idaho town's study that is most widely quoted. These more accurate surveys suggest some implications: (a) *Socio-economic factors are important.* In communities where cars for teen-agers are taken for granted, possessing a car and driving it does not usually affect grades if the parents pay for the car and its upkeep. If, on the other hand, the youngster must buy his own car and pay the operation and maintenance costs, he is likely to neglect his school work to support the car. (b) *Academic abilities are important.* Students who are outstanding scholastically tend to remain so when they have cars. Students who fail or almost fail because of low academic ability continue to fail subjects at which they have never been able to succeed, much less excel. They buy a car, get a job to support it, fail in school, drop out. As Dr. Wahlquist suggests, the dull-normal student's devotion to a car is often a *symptom* of his failure in school, rarely the cause of it.

This is not to say, of course, that all students who drop out of school to support an automobile have dull-normal intelligence. On the contrary, the Allstate Insurance Company's survey, which included seventy-five high schools across the nation, indicates that the very bright student with exceptionally high grades who goes suddenly "car-crazy" is the one who is likely to suffer most. His grades may drop from A to C, D, or F. To conclude that the automobile *causes* this kind of behavior is to commit a serious error in diagnosis. Actually, this youngster's sudden devotion to a car and his utter disregard for school work that he viewed previously as being important constitute symptoms of *emotional disturbance.* If the boy had not gone "car-crazy," he would probably have lost himself suddenly in some other activity and ignored his school work just the same.

Allstate's survey, which supports in general all other surveys except the Idaho one, concludes that cars do not necessarily cause poor school work. The student who has little or no interest in school work gets interested in a car often as a diversion from boredom. The junior high school student who gets a car suffers the greatest scholastic drop. The student who has owned a car the longest time tends to have the worst grades. Students who hold a job to support a car have the poorest grades of all. Students who have neither a car nor a job are twice as likely to be receiving A and B grades as are those who work and own a car. Students who drive cars only on weekends do not suffer any drop in grades. Students who drive two days of the five-day school week are less than half as likely to be D or F students as students who use a car four days a week.

Findings cited from the Allstate study have important implications for parents: (a) Youngsters should usually not own a car unless they need one for a specific purpose or purposes, (b) Delay the teen-agers' owning a car as long as is feasible, (c) It is usually a mistake to expect a high school teen-ager to buy a car, pay operation and maintenance costs. Parents should ordinarily be responsible for this expense if it must be incurred, (d) Scholarship should come first, cars later. If the teen-ager's grades drop when he has a car, withdraw permission to drive until he does better in school, (e) Restrict the use of cars to weekends whenever feasible.

Measure your youngster's competence as a driver against adult standards. Recently, a penitent father stood begging leniency for his seventeen-year-old son, who, driving his father's car, had run a boulevard stop, plunged broadside into a stationwagon loaded with children, killed the mother who was driving and three of the children, injuring the rest. "Your Honor," the father said, his eyes red from weeping, "what my boy did was wrong. But it was an accident, Your Honor. John is a good boy; he would never do anything like that on purpose. And, Your Honor, please remember: he's only a boy."

" 'Only a boy,' " the judge said painfully. "Any young man who's only a boy has no business sitting behind the wheel of a powerful automobile. No one belongs there who does not at all times perform as if he were completely grown-up."

The teen-ager who drives on modern America's streets and highways assumes adult responsibility; he holds in his hands other people's lives as well as his own. He is responsible for using wisely the privilege of driving a car. If his performance suggests that he regards this privilege lightly, misuses or abuses it, the teen-ager's driver's license should be suspended.

Teen-age drivers are privileged equally under the law with adult drivers. Their cars go as fast, travel as far, kill or maim more than their share; consequently, teenagers should be held to account for their performance behind the wheel as if they were in fact grown-up.

Recognize your parental responsibilities; play your parent role wisely. Parents are liable ordinarily for their teen-ager's damage to persons or property while he is driving his own car or the family car. The parent cannot legally relinquish this responsibility to the youngster; he should not, under any circumstances, relinquish it in the moral sense. The parent owns the car keys as well as the car; he should retain them, if necessary, to fulfill his responsibility as the car's owner and the teen-ager's protector. He himself must decide when his youngster merits the privilege of driving; he must withdraw that privilege when necessary, modify it as circumstances indicate. Here are some suggestions, based on recent research, that parents may find helpful.

1. If feasible, withhold extensive car privileges until your teen-ager is seventeen years old or older. Give only incidental privileges to sixteen-year-olds.

2. Have a clear understanding with your teen-ager regarding the days, hours, and circumstances under which he may use the car, those under which he must not use it.

3. Never permit your youngster to drive—even to back the car out of the garage—without a valid driver's license. If he has a learner's permit, the same rule holds except when there is a licensed driver beside him in conformity with the law.

4. Insist that your teen-age driver know the state vehicle code. He may obtain a copy of it free from the state motor vehicle department; he should study it until he knows it.

5. Insist that your youngster obey traffic regulations.

6. If your teen-age driver gets a traffic citation, let him take the full consequences of his error. This way he will profit most from his mistake.

7. If your youngster is cited repeatedly for traffic violations, consider this pattern an indication either of incompetence as a driver or of emotional instability. Then act accordingly. If he is incompetent as a driver, he should be grounded. If he is emotionally unstable, he may be using the automobile as a weapon for revenge against authority, in which case he should be grounded and referred for psychological study. (Studies have shown that repeat violators are usually in trouble with themselves.)

8. Rules regarding use of the family car for dates were discussed on pages 82-84. Enforce these rules rather rigidly.

9. The parent holds final authority in all matters pertaining to the car, even if it is the youngster's. Exercise that authority wisely and well.

Be sure your teen-ager's car is mechanically safe and sound. The emotional factors in driving have been considered rather carefully; the mechanical features of the automobile are, without doubt, equally important. Several major researches (Columbia University; Cornell University; Allstate Insurance; and others) have shown that . certain mechanical features in automobiles increase the occupants' safety: seat belts, good ones, attached firmly to the floor of the car; padded dashboard; padded sun visors; steering wheel with malleable recessed spokes; safety locks on the doors; brakes in good order; steering mechanism in good order; tires good and sound; lights sound and working; directional signals in good working order; shock absorbers working effectively. Check these items carefully on your youngster's car and your own.

Insist that your youngster use the safety devices that are available in the car. The National Safety Council declares that if all occupants of automobiles were to wear effective seat belts at all times, the death rate from automobile accidents would be cut in half and nonfatal injuries would be reduced 60 to 80 per cent. Use of seat belts in cars has been publicly endorsed by the American Medical Association, the American College of Surgeons, the United States Public Health Service—conservative organizations that extend endorsements only on proof that is convincing. Yet, in 1961, only one car in a hundred throughout the nation was equipped with seat belts; furthermore, many occupants of cars equipped with seat belts did not use them, as accident analyses proved. A recent study of crashes revealed, for example, that only 20 per cent of the people who had seat belts in the car had them fastened at the time of the accident; 80 per cent were not using them.

Your car and your teen-ager's car, if he has one, should be equipped with seat belts that are used whenever the car is in motion. The belt must be adequate (5,000-pound tested) and solidly anchored to the steel floor structure with reinforcing plates or, in older cars, to the frame.

The National Safety Council reports also that, contrary to public opinion, most traffic fatalities are *not* caused by excessive speed. In reality, half of all fatalities from automobile accidents result from cars traveling at speeds *less than forty miles an hour.* Many fatalities result from occupants' being crushed against the steering wheel, bounced off the windshield, otherwise slammed about, or by being thrown out of the car. Seat belts and safety locks on the doors could play important roles in such accidents. Seat belts hold drivers in their seats so they may retain control of the car; they hold all the car's occupants firmly in place, avoid bumps and bruises. Safety locks keep car doors from flying open; otherwise, occupants who are not secured by seat belts may be thrown out of the car on impact of collision. The chances for surviving an accident, the National Safety Council reports, are forty per cent better when the person remains inside the car, where he escapes injuries commonly sustained by encountering, unprotected, a curb, a tree, a lamppost, or the pavement.

If your teen-ager has a car, encourage him to join a car club. Teen-age boys who own cars tend to associate closely with one another. They may organize a car club, formulate rules, elect officers, hold meetings. Such clubs may be undesirable when they are without responsible adult guidance and supervision. Properly administered, however, they are usually quite beneficial.

Car clubs operate best when they are sponsored by an organization or institution, such as a men's service club, the police department, or the highway safety department. Such sponsorship usually makes a club into a very good one. The Cobra Car Club of San Marino (California) High School, for example, whose members traditionally assist motorists in distress, made such an outstanding record in its first six years that two additional clubs were formed with the approval and encouragement of the San Marino Police Department. The rules of these clubs are very strict. Any member of a police-recognized club is automatically expelled, for example, if cited for drag racing or for reckless driving.

The San Marino Police Department reports that teen-agers' membership in constructive car clubs has resulted in dramatic reductions in frequency of juvenile traffic citations. The first year the Cobra Club existed, citations of its members dropped 70 per cent; by the end of the sixth year, this figure had reached 90 per cent. Frequent letters to the editors of local and metropolitan newspapers from grateful motorists who had been helped by members of the Cobra Club, always without remuneration, indicate clearly the wholesome, constructive nature of the youngsters' activities on streets and highways.

Car clubs such as this one hold inspections regularly, opening their cars from stem to stern to public view and to the discerning eyes of experts from the state highway department. Brakes, steering mechanisms, suspension systems, engines, transmissions, clutches, safety belts, safety locks, and other mechanical components are gone over bit by bit for wear and possible failure. Tires must show at least one-eighth inch of tread. Each car must have seat belts anchored to frame members, with approved super-safe linkage. Roll-over bars are equipped on sports roadsters, which must also be equipped with crash helmets for driver and passengers alike. No car passes inspection that has a fuel, water, grease, or oil leak. Cars must be kitchen clean from bumper to bumper before inspectors will look at them. Any car with a dirty engine or undercarriage is refused inspection until it is clean. "A similar check-up and safety equipment program for the general public's cars," a National Safety Council official declares, "would save thousands of lives from auto accidents each year."

Driving skill, not "driving madness," marks the con-structive car clubs' joint meetings. The obstacle course illustrates this point. Clubs join together periodically under police or state highway patrol supervision, set up an obstacle course on a spacious, paved area, such as a huge parking lot. Teen-agers drive their cars through the ob-stacle course, trying to negotiate the course with a minimum number of errors. The emphasis is on accuracy. The cars move very slowly and carefully, with great precision. Awards are made to the youngsters who maneuver the course with a minimum number of errors. This training helps save lives on America's streets and highways.

Subscribe to a publication that stresses safe driving, proper care and treatment of automobiles. Many publications about cars and safe driving contain valuable suggestions for teen-agers. Periodicals about cars are available on most magazine racks. In addition, automobile manufacturers may provide guides for young drivers. General Motors Corporation (Detroit, Michigan), for example, publishes an attractive bi-monthly magazine, *American Youth,* and sends it free to newly licensed drivers. This magazine features well-presented articles on safe driving habits interspersed with short pieces by and about interesting teen-agers. It is wisely not top-heavy with the moralistic preachments most teen-agers resent. It is available to young drivers on request.

Set your youngster a good example in your own driving habits. Teen-agers who seem accident-prone and those who receive many citations for traffic violations are often in conflict with their parents, according to many researches. The parents tend generally to be autocratic, dictatorial: they "lay down the law," preach to the teen-ager, give him no opportunity to express his own feelings. The youngster gets in his car angrily, vents his hostility by speeding, bluffs his way through traffic. He is discourteous, defies authority openly. Psychiatrists say he is "acting out" in his car the anger he feels inside for his parents.

Perhaps the best brief answer to this problem is this: parents are wise who themselves drive intelligently and safely, who teach teen-agers by example rather than by preaching, who give advice only when it is appropriate, worthwhile, and genuinely needed.

If your youngster continues getting into trouble in spite of your efforts to help, take away his car and his driving privilege; that is your parental responsibility. Then seek professional help for him and for your own inadequate parent-child relationship.

Review of major points

1. Recognize the important role of the automobile in the United States.
2. Encourage your teen-ager to take behind-the-wheel driver training.
3. Appreciate the hazards automobiles pose to young people.
4. Understand the teen-ager's desire to drive and own a car.
5. Appreciate the emotional factors in teen-age driving.
6. Help your youngster view cars in proper perspective.
7. Reconcile school, jobs, and driving.
8. Measure your youngster's competence as a driver against adult standards.
9. Recognize your parental responsibilities; play your parental role wisely.
10. Be sure your teen-ager's car is mechanically safe and sound.
11. Insist that your youngster use the safety devices that are available in the car.
12. If your teen-ager has a car, encourage him to join a constructive car club.
13. Subscribe to a publication that stresses safe driving, proper care and treatment of automobiles.
14. Set your youngster a good example in your own driving habits.

SUMMARY

This chapter discussed automobiles in the lives of adolescents and suggested ways in which parents can help their teen-ager view automobiles realistically and operate them safely.

The next chapter will discuss education during adolescence and suggest ways parents can help their teen-ager get the most benefit from secondary school.

Chapter 10

School

THE UNITED STATES stands alone among the nations of the world in the education of children and youth: universal, free, compulsory school attendance is provided for all educable persons, generally from eight years old to sixteen; and, in addition, permissive, free, universal schooling beyond this age range, beginning generally before the child is five years old and continuing into adulthood.

The public schools of America, whose primary purpose is to make an intelligent citizenry, are the most comprehensive, the most complex, the most all-inclusive in the world. They are the most admired, the most highly praised, the most frequently imitated schools in the world. They are at the same time the most widely criticized, the most thoroughly maligned, the most vulnerable to attack of all educational institutions on earth. Such is the nature of public education in our democratic way of life: large, free, seemingly inefficient, yet remarkably productive.

Educating America's children and youth is a task almost too great to comprehend. In America's public high schools of 1960, for example, there were almost 11,000,000 students. The number continues to grow each year. How may such vast numbers of young people go to school and yet maintain their individual identities? How may the curriculum provide for individual differences that exist among students? How may youngsters' aptitudes and interests, strengths and weaknesses, talents and skills be identified, directed, utilized intelligently for their own good and for the good of the nation? How may teen-age boys and girls be taught to live and learn together in harmony, wholesomely, intelligently, without going too far in social-sexual involvements? How may they be persuaded to be honest, fair-minded citizens—tomorrow's leaders, parents, patriots? How may they be stimulated to work to their maximum capacity, to utilize the intellectual endowments

God gave them, to produce the most that is in their power to achieve? These are but a few of the problems that loom large in the minds of America's parents and educators.

These are difficult problems. Educators cannot solve them alone. They need parents' help.

What may you do to help your teen-ager be successful in school? The suggestions that follow are guidelines.

Understand and appreciate your community's schools. Studies indicate that the children whose parents know their schools, are interested in them, and participate actively in parent-teacher and other home-school-community programs are usually quite successful in school. Parental support of the schools does not necessarily cause children's school success, but the two factors are associated. Parents' attitudes are contagious to children; therefore, children usually adopt their parents' faith in public schools and want to be successful. Conversely, parents who reject the schools pass this attitude on to their youngsters, encourage them to react negatively, motivate them to fail. Perhaps the most important way you can help your teen-ager get the most out of school is to support the school yourself. Expect it to meet his needs, to bring out his finest qualities. If you really believe in the school, it will probably do just that.

Encourage your youngster to do his best in school. People get the most out of life who give the most to it. The same principle holds for your teen-ager in school: he will profit from school in proportion to the enthusiasm, effort, and energy he puts into it. It is to his advantage and yours when he directs his academic energies positively, constructively.

Parents are wise who praise their youngsters for school-work they have done well, who show by their approving attitude that they believe in them, trust them, expect them always to do their best. It is a mistake, however, to give material rewards—money, gifts, prizes, etc.—for making good grades in school. To do so provides artificial, un-desirable motives that are likely to make the youngster self-centered, egocentric. Furthermore, offering material rewards is a form of bribery in which the teen-ager himself holds the controlling reins: if he is to be paid, he produces, if he is not to be paid, he loafs. Working for good marks to win a school award or to make an honor roll poses similarly artificial motivation and should not be encouraged.

Motivation to learn should derive from the youngster's genuine interest in the subject matter and his long-term objective. If John hopes some day to become a physician, he will probably find biology, chemistry, physics and other significant courses especially interesting. If he does so, he should strive to master them. If, on the other hand, he finds them too difficult, too boring, too far removed from his true interests and enthusiasms, this discovery may signal that he is aspiring to enter a field of work that is probably wrong for him. If this is true, he should not force himself to earn high marks in these classes even if doing so would mean winning a prize. Furthermore, his parents add to his confusion if they urge him continually to achieve.

"Doing one's best in school" does not necessarily mean making all A's or all A's and B's. It does mean putting one's best abilities to use within the limitations of the school program, doing so with zest and enthusiasm, employing natural creativity and special talents in every way possible. If outstanding marks result from the process, well and good. If, on the other hand, one "does his best" in these ways and still brings home C's, he should probably be considered successful in spite of the marks.

If you think your teen-ager is not doing as well as he should be doing in school, talk with his counselor or adviser.

Accept your teen-ager's mental abilities. Most parents judge a youngster's mental abilities rather accurately, recognize his special talents, perceive his strengths and weaknesses, especially when they have other children with whom to compare him. Some parents, however, overestimate or underestimate their youngster's ability to achieve in school and are not aware of his hidden potentialities, his strengths, his weaknesses. They are often too close to the youngster, both emotionally and physically, to view him objectively. School personnel, on the other hand, see him as one of many hundreds of boys and girls. They recognize characteristics and patterns of behavior in him that parents may miss until they are pointed out. Furthermore, teachers sometimes regard certain traits as normal that parents believe are distinctly negative and possibly abnormal. Thus, parents find that talking with teachers about their youngster and his problems is often a helpful, enlightening experience.

Studies suggest that 80 per cent of all parents think their youngster is above average mentally. Some of these parents must be wrong, since only 50 per cent of all youngsters are above the mean (average), and the other 50 per cent are below it. Many parents are keenly disappointed when they learn that their child does not measure up to their expectations.

The terms average and normal as applied to tests of mental ability refer usually to the middle two-thirds of the population. This group includes all testees who make an intelligence quotient (I. Q. score) between 90 and 109. The remaining one-third of the population is divided equally, half of them being above normal, the other half below normal; thus, one-sixth of the population is in each of these categories. These two groups are divided further: the below normal group includes dull-normal, mentally retarded, and severely mentally retarded; the above normal group includes above normal, superior, and gifted. Categories and percentages vary among mental abilities tests; they are, however, roughly as follows:

Category	IQ.	Percentage of Population
Gifted	140 and up	1 per cent
Superior	125-140	3 per cent
Above normal	110-124	13 per cent
Normal	90-109	67 per cent
Dull-Normal	76-89	13 per cent
Mentally retarded	50-75	2 per cent
Severely retarded	30-49	1 per cent

Public schools are generally geared to the normal students, reaching upward often to satisfy those who are above normal. Many of them do not challenge adequately the superior students, who find the work too easy to hold their interest. Gifted students breeze through school with even less effort, and get their best education, in some instances, not at school but elsewhere in the community and at home. Highly gifted students, who score extremely high scores on individual intelligence tests, are far beyond the ordinary school curriculum, in which they are normally "misfits." They refuse sometimes to study at all because the assignments are too simple. They fail sometimes in school because they refuse to conform to the rules.

There is clearly a need for special education, for enrichment of the curriculum and other measures to make life at school more meaningful and challenging to superior, gifted, and highly gifted students. Such education is imperative if the nation is to stop wasting much of its top potential talent. If your youngsters falls into these upper categories, discuss the problem with school officials, and ask them about the CEEB Advanced Placement Program.[1]

Students who have below average mental ability may make low marks or fail in school because the work is either too difficult for them or because the subjects do not interest them. These youngsters earn mostly C's, D's, and some F's. They get discouraged easily, create problems often for school authorities by being truant, belligerent, resentful. They are the ones most likely to drop out of school as soon as they are old enough under the law. These youngsters need a school program that fits their needs, a program that few high schools provide. If your youngster is in this category, urge the school authorities to provide an appropriate curriculum for him and other students who are below average but not mentally retarded. At the same time, praise your youngster

[1] Information about this program may be obtained on request from the Director, Advanced Placement Program, College Entrance Examination Board, 475 Riverside Drive, New York 27, New York.

for his achievements, limited as they may be. Let him know he is wanted, loved, appreciated.

Boys and girls who are mentally retarded have usually been identified long before they reach secondary schools and in most states have been segregated for special education and training. This arrangement is necessary and beneficial to the youngsters and to society.

It is important that you know your youngster's level of mental ability, whether he is in the normal group, below normal, gifted, or what-have-you. Your expectations for your teen-ager in school and in society should be in harmony with his mental abilities, aptitudes, talents, strengths and weaknesses.

If you are seriously in doubt about your youngster's abilities, consult a qualified psychologist who will study him and give you an objective evaluation. Before you do this, however, discuss your concerns with school personnel to learn what test information they have about your teenager that they may share with you.

Encourage your teen-ager to use the school guidance and counseling services. Most school districts today have guidance programs that begin when the child enters kindergarten and continue until he completes high school or drops out. Standardized group tests of reading readiness, achievement in the fundamental subjects (reading, arithmetic, general information), mental maturity, interests, aptitudes, and mastery of specific subjects are usually used. These tests provide objective data that help school persons evaluate a youngster's abilities and performance in relation to other persons his age or grade level. They are not infallible; yet they are helpful, practical, and feasible for use with large numbers of students.

A student's test results and expert interpretations of them are usually available to parents who make an appointment with the appropriate person—usually the school counselor. A parent-counselor conference is usually extremely helpful in clarifying the parent's own mental image of his teen-ager.

Parents of elementary school children go to school regularly and spontaneously for conferences and other home-school affairs, and the youngsters are almost always delighted to see them there. Parents of junior high and senior high school students face a more difficult situation, however, because youngsters this age prefer that parents stay away from school. Parents' being at school suggests (in the youngster's mind) that the teen-ager is still a child, quite incapable of taking care of himself. Therefore, parents should go to secondary schools only by prearranged appointments. Furthermore, they should be inconspicuous to students while there and depart without attracting attention. Parents should tell their teen-ager beforehand when they will be at school, whom they will see, what they expect to discuss. This way he knows the parents' intentions and feels they are lending him moral support.

Parents who talk with their youngster's counselor should be especially careful not to ask for information that might be considered confidential and privileged. Many teen-agers say things to the counselor that they would not say to anyone else—their opinions of teachers, their own feelings of inadequacy, their feelings about the principal or the coach, their attitudes toward their own parents. They want to let off steam without being reprimanded for their thoughts, and counselors are usually good listeners who respect students' feelings, justified or not. A competent, ethical counselor does not repeat anything told to him in confidence by a student. Therefore, parents should not ask such questions as these: "How does Johnny feel about his father—or mother, or Uncle Charlie, or Aunt Jane?" "Does Johnny ever tell you about the girl he is determined to marry when he graduates from high school?" "Johnny never tells us about his friends at school. Do you know them?" The counselor would probably jeopardize his relationship with Johnny if he answered such questions.

Johnny would not trust him again if he found out. Granted that parents should know answers to such questions; however, it is not fair to ask them of the counselor. Parents should always assure the teen-ager that they do not "snoop" when they talk with his counselor.

Encourage your teen-ager to get along well with teachers and other school personnel. Elementary school pupils have one teacher all day, week after week, the entire school year. They get to know her very well. If they love her, they are fortunate; if they do not like her, they suffer perhaps too long. In junior high and senior high school, however, students have several teachers, a different one perhaps for each subject. They formulate quickly their impressions of teachers: Mary likes Mrs. Jones; Nancy thinks she is too strict. Jerry thinks Mr. Harrison is a swell teacher, but Walter thinks he is arrogant. Kathy says, "All the kids like Miss Quimby, but no one can stand Miss Severe—she's too mean."

Getting acquainted with many different teachers helps teen-agers grow up. Youngsters at this age are moving away gradually from their parents; consequently, they project their inner feelings often onto teachers, attributing to them qualities—good or evil—that perhaps are not there at all. Thus, Mary perceives Mrs. Jones as "real dreamy"; in reality, Mrs. Jones is a plain, energetic, ordinary (on the surface, at least) young woman. Jerry sees Mr. Harrison as brave, self-sacrificing, the hero type; Walter says angrily, "The guy's a bore, a stupid square with a swollen head." Obviously, the teacher cannot be all the personalities whom students project. He is wise when he tries to be merely himself and hopes for the best.

Teen-agers think unconsciously sometimes of the teacher as a parent substitute, a man who is like (or unlike) Father or a woman who is like (or unlike) Mother. Occasionally, this attitude manifests itself dramatically. Recently, for example, sixteen-year-old Randy, a competent, hard-working student assaulted Mr. Bass, his mathematics teacher, knocking him to the floor and kicking him viciously for no apparent reason. Mr. Bass was at a loss to explain Randy's behavior; the boy had always been quiet, polite, well-behaved in class. Randy refused to talk about the incident; the school principal turned him over, therefore, to juvenile authorities. Later, in juvenile court, Randy explained to the referee: "Mr. Bass called me 'a lazy bum.' That's what my dad calls me all the time at home. I have to take it from my dad, but I don't have to take it from Mr. Bass or anyone else at school." Mr. Bass could not recall having made such a remark to Randy. "But if I did call him 'a lazy bum,' " Mr. Bass explained, "I was joking. Randy is a good boy. He's a hard worker— I have never for a moment thought him lazy."

This is not to say, of course, that all teen-agers' opinions of teachers are products of their own fantasies. Teachers differ just as other persons differ in personal and vocational effectiveness. Most of them are, by definition, normal or average. Some are superior, some are inferior. A few are gifted; a few are, unfortunately, quite incompetent. Consequently, one should listen to youngsters' comments about their teachers and evaluate them with an open mind.

Adolescents usually prefer teachers who are friendly, cheerful, sociable; who are honest, sincere, fair-minded; who treat all students alike, have no favorites; who know their subject matter extremely well and communicate it effectively; who are rather strict in the classroom; who give challenging assignments and expect the students to do them promptly and well; who genuinely like teen-agers and enjoy being with them; who respect everyone and are respected in return; who listen patiently, sympathetically to students and help them with their problems.

Adolescents ordinarily reject teachers whose personal qualities are opposite to those of the teachers whom they like. They do not like the teacher who is "crabby" or "grouchy"; who has favorites; who grades unfairly; who does not know his subject; who cannot teach his subject effectively; who assigns useless "busy work"; who is a poor disciplinarian—either too strict or not strict enough;

who does not like teen-agers; who is impolite, disrespectful to others and is treated the same in return; who is not interested in teen-agers or their problems.[2]

Most teachers do not fit either of these categories exclusively; rather they are somewhere in between the two extremes. Teen-agers usually think "average" teachers are "okay"; they can, as a rule, take them or leave them.

If your teen-ager likes most of his teachers, consider this attitude a sign of his own security as well as of the teachers' competence. If, on the other hand, he complains too much about them, try to find out who is at fault, your youngster or his teachers. You may discover his classmates' reactions to a teacher by talking with their parents. A preliminary investigation such as this should ordinarily precede any visit you might make to school.

Support school personnel in disciplinary procedures. Young people today have apparently less respect for authority than their grandparents did when they were teen-agers. Many factors contribute to this attitude: freedom to move about rapidly, especially in cars; increased rights and privileges for women and girls; increased freedom and rivalry between the sexes; legislation that protects children and youth from too severe punishment by adults; movies, television, radio, telephone, books, newspapers and other mass media of communication; war and threats of war; compulsory military training for older teen-agers; wide-spread use of tobacco and alcohol; increased use of drugs and narcotics; increasingly complex society; and others.

Newspapers emphasize usually the sensational side of teen-agers' misbehavior: delinquency, crime, violence, drug addiction. *The Blackboard Jungle* by Evan Hunter and similar books have created the public impression that

[2] The generalizations regarding teen-agers' positive and negative reactions to teachers are based on the findings of several researches, the first and most important of which is reported in *Teachers and Teaching,* by Frank W. Hart, Ph.D. (New York: Macmillan and Co., 1934). This study was conducted almost two generations ago; yet subsequent studies consistently validate Hart's findings, prove them universally accurate today.

many modern teen-agers are so vicious they will hardly permit a teacher to enter the classroom, that the teacher who goes to school unarmed risks his very life. Such schools do exist. However, they are not typical public schools; they are the exception, not the rule. Nor are undisciplined students—the truants, the delinquents, the violent ones— typical American teen-agers. On the contrary, they are emotionally disturbed youngsters who need psychiatric treatment and who must have it if they are ever to profit substantially from school or make worthwhile contributions to society.

Emotionally disturbed teen-agers, small in number but large in the public mind, have given public secondary schools a distorted reputation that is not generally justified. Some citizens, puzzled and fearful, demand a return to corporal punishment for adolescents who misbehave in school; they think flogging teen-agers will bring them into line. Most people—especially parents—realize that this approach to the problem would solve nothing, but would create new problems instead; therefore, they wisely turn their backs on such proposals.

Teachers in public schools are in an unenviable position: they must teach boys and girls from all walks of life, from varying home backgrounds, including many adolescents who do not want to be in school and some who probably should not be there. They establish rules and regulations, often with the advice and consent of the students—a sound democratic procedure. They may fall short, however, when enforcement of rules and regulations requires more than polite pressure. Teachers are strictly regulated by law; they cannot exercise legally certain privileges a parent enjoys in disciplining his children. Most parents want it that way, according to opinion polls, and teachers do too.

Parents should teach their youngsters to obey school rules and regulations, to respect and comply with the stated wishes of school personnel. When teen-agers break the school's rules, they should be willing to accept disciplinary action; that is the way it is in the adult community when one breaks society's rules. Parents who support the school when their teen-ager gets in trouble help him learn a lesson in good citizenship. Parents who, on the other hand, defend the youngster when he breaks the rules teach him unwittingly to become a second-rate citizen. Parents should assume that the school is right and their teen-ager is wrong until they have ample evidence that the opposite situation prevails. Only then should they move in the teen-ager's defense.

Give your youngster enough educational support. Parents' attitudes toward education largely determine the teen-ager's feelings about school work and create the atmosphere in which he studies at home. Parents who value education highly transmit this positive attitude to their youngsters and encourage them to learn at home as well as at school.

Knowing how to study effectively is often the determining factor in academic success. Parents can help their youngsters study effectively at home by observing such rules as these:

Provide a place for study. A teen-ager needs a place of his own to study. If he has his own room, it is probably the best place. The room should be equipped with a desk, chair, lamp, bookrack, textbooks, reference books, dictionary, paper, and other paraphernalia that he needs.

Provide a time for study. Help your teen-ager work out a regular weekly time schedule for study. This means scheduling through and around television programs, extracurricular activities, and other distractions. Study periods should be neither too long nor too brief.

Provide an atmosphere for learning. Most people study best when it is quiet, when no one else is present to interrupt. Some students study effectively with background music (radio, record player), while others are distracted by it. No one can watch TV and study at the same time, since TV requires both visual and auditory attention. The television set in the study room should therefore be turned off during study periods.

Help your teen-ager recognize the value of study. Study is not an end in itself; rather, it is a means to an end. If your youngster sees no purpose to study, help him discover the significance of the subject he is studying and the ways he may use it now and in the future.

Answer your teen-agers' questions if you can. Ideas and concepts that adults take for granted are often new and challenging to adolescents, stimulate them intellectually, cause them to ask many questions. Parents should be patient, give plausible explanations; they should also encourage their youngsters to think, to look up answers in reference books, to search for deeper meanings beneath the surface of the subjects they are studying.

Relate school subjects to the wider community. Adults who know what subjects their teen-ager is studying in school can add to his knowledge and enthusiasm by talking about related experiences, taking him on field trips, suggesting activities that would supplement the school work. For example, family discussion of world events helps the youngster understand history; a trip to the science exhibit helps bring science courses to life; an evening at the theatre helps the youngster appreciate drama and literature.

Encourage the school to offer training in study habits. Knowing how to study effectively is often an important causal factor in academic success in college. Dr. George Weigand of the University of Maryland says, "At least 90 per cent of the freshman students who come here don't know how to study effectively. The toll of those who don't make the grade in college because they don't know how to study is tragic. Approximately 40 per cent of the young men and women who start college never finish; about half of these students fail academically or, in their words, they 'flunk out.' Many students who 'flunk out' have adequate intelligence, but they have not been taught how to study effectively.

"Study skills should be taught in the high school, but they aren't. Some private prep schools have courses in how to study, but you will find them in only a handful of public schools."

I agree with Dr. Weigand that all secondary schools should teach students how to study effectively since few parents are able to do this. Instructional units ordinarily include such items as these: budgeting time, learning to read faster and with greater comprehension, reading for meaning, reviewing for mastery, taking notes during lectures and from reading, spacing study periods, using drill for mastery, improving memory, using problem-solving techniques, studying for examinations, taking examinations. Students who have been trained in study skills have an advantage over those who have not had such training. If your youngster's school does not provide such training, you may want to suggest it to school authorities.

Appreciate the value of co-curricular and extracurricular school activities. Most modern secondary schools have a vast program of co-curricular activities, which relate directly to subjects being studied in school, and extracurricular activities, which do not relate directly to subject matter. Science clubs, drama clubs, writers' clubs and educational field trips are examples of co-curricular activities. Athletic contests, school plays and school dances are examples of extracurricular activities. Both types of activities are usually valuable for most teen-agers.

Many parents think extracurricular activities are given too much emphasis in today's secondary schools. They would like less emphasis on competitive interscholastic sports—football, basketball, baseball, etc.—and more emphasis on academic achievement. They think teen-agers spend too much time and energy dating, dancing, going to parties, and too little time studying at home. They are undoubtedly justified in some cases. Yet the parents themselves and other adults serve as models whom the youngsters imitate. Adolescents' preoccupation with competitive sports, social engagements, and having a good time reflects the adult culture. Adults, especially male alumni, want competitive sports; furthermore, they want their school's team to win. Female adults want to be popular, admired, socially adept, and they want their daughters to be the same.

The best solution to the problem is probably to accept extracurricular school activities as valuable experiences, as means to ends, not as ends in themselves. A football game is a football game—no more, no less. It may seem important at the moment, but tomorrow it will be forgotten. Academic achievement, on the other hand, means something personal to the student and forecasts still greater achievements throughout life. Intelligent, healthy-minded, socially competent adolescents who understand this difference can participate normally in extracurricular activities and do their school work well too.

Discourage teen-agers' joining illegal secret clubs and societies. Several years ago, thousands of high school students throughout the nation organized secret clubs, many of them recognizable imitations of college sororities and fraternities. These clubs shared certain common characteristics: restricted membership; closed (secret) meetings; identifying insignia, such as pins, sweaters, coats of arms; exclusive social affairs; primary allegiance of the members; hazing initiations. These clubs were undemocratic, members being flagrantly chosen on the basis of creed, color, economic status, family prominence rather than on personal abilities, achievements, or interests. They produced cliques, factions, rivalries and jealousies among adolescent boys and girls and among their parents, who were either attracted or disturbed by the clubs' "snob appeal." The clubs were generally without adequate adult supervision and were entirely independent of the school. Yet they disrupted the school activity program by fostering members' allegiance to the clubs rather than to the school. Members voted for fellow club members for student government posts rather than voting for the qualified candidate. On the football field, club members played favorites, caused teammates who were members of rival clubs to look inept. Thus, the secret clubs rendered ineffective the lessons in responsible citizenship, good sportsmanship, and fair play that the school was trying to teach.

High school secret clubs multiplied and became such a nuisance that many states and local school boards declared them illegal, penalized students who joined them by excluding them from extracurricular activities, denying them a diploma, or expelling them from school. Several lawsuits were filed against high schools by irate parents, who charged that the school's position constituted a violation of personal rights, an invasion of parental authority, unwarranted paternalism, cruel or unusual punishment, unconstitutional discrimination, or unreasonable procedure. In each case the court upheld the school, ruling the parent's position untenable. The court believes generally that individuals (teen-agers, in this instance) who seek the benefits of the state's educational institutions must submit to all reasonable regulations imposed on students.

I have gone into considerable detail about the history of high school societies because, although illegal, *they still exist in large numbers.* They are usually promoted by teenagers and *supported, in spirit at least, by their parents,* who know they are illegal, yet permit their youngsters to join so they may be with the "right" crowd. In doing so, they teach their teen-agers unwittingly to break the law, to oppose the school program, to become social snobs.

Wise parents teach their children to be good citizens in school and in the wider community. If your youngster gets an invitation to join a high school club, be sure it is an authorized organization, approved by the board of education, and subject to supervision by school personnel. Otherwise, you may be giving him a passport to trouble when you give your consent.

Encourage your youngster to stay in school until he completes his education. The fifty states of our nation provide universal, free education from the first grade through the twelfth and require attendance by law in certain age ranges. Yet, in spite of this excellent opportunity, *four out of ten youngsters in America today do not graduate from high school.* Some of them never get to high school; they drop out during elementary school. Others start high school but drop out, do not complete the requirements for a diploma.

Why do forty per cent of America's teen-agers leave school? There are many reasons: failure in studies, dull-normal intelligence, lack of interest in school work, inadequate or inappropriate curriculum, disinterested parents, boredom at school, desire or need to get a job and earn money. Bright students drop out of school but at a lesser rate than dull students. Similarly, students from upper- and middle-class homes drop out at a lesser rate than lower-class students.

How may you know if your youngster is thinking about dropping out of school? He may simply tell you he wants to drop out. Otherwise, you may want to compare him with the typical adolescent who does drop out.

The potential high school drop-out tends to reject school, competition, and himself. He feels generally frustrated and insecure at school. He stays out of school often and is frequently tardy. He makes poor grades, has trouble with some teachers. He feels socially unaccepted and inadequate. He has a few friends. He does not participate in extracurricular activities. He doubts his ability to succeed in school and wonders whether he will be able to make a living when his school days are over. He does not go to church nor belong to a religious youth group. His parents are not particularly concerned about his educational future; they do not really care whether he stays in school or drops out.[3]

This composite word-picture suggests that the drop-out

---

[3] The typical drop-out's description was constructed from data in *Motivations of Youth for Leaving School* (Cooperative Research Project No. 200), by Paul H. Bowman and Charles V. Matthews (Washington, D.C.: United States Office of Education, 1960).

feels utterly hopeless. Yet many students who are intellectually able to complete high school and perhaps to go through college drop out because their parents do not insist that they remain in school. Studies show conclusively that parents' aspirations for their child help decide the youngster's educational plans more clearly than any other factor or combination of factors. An individual's educational future thus appears to be more firmly in his parents' minds and hands than in his own.

There are many reasons for encouraging a teen-ager not to drop out of school. He is too young to be needed on the labor market; furthermore, he is untrained, unskilled, uneducated. He is too young to get married, as the dramatic divorce rate among teen-age couples suggests. He would limit his primary social relationships to other drop-outs and adults. He would probably never return to school to resume his studies. By leaving school he would greatly increase statistically his chances for getting in trouble with the law.

Parents who encourage their teen-agers to remain in school until they have completed all educational prerequisites for their vocation or profession and for successful living do them a very great favor.

Investigate the school work-study program as it pertains to your teen-ager. Many high schools have a program in which a student works part time in a firm outside the school and receives credit toward graduation. There are several types of work-study programs; each has certain advantages. Since work, vocational education, and money management—the key elements in high school work-study programs—are the subjects of the next chapter, work-study programs will be explained and discussed there.

Review of major points

1. Understand and appreciate your community's schools.
2. Encourage your youngster to do his best in school.
3. Accept your teen-ager's mental abilities.

4. Encourage your teen-ager to use the school guidance and counseling services.
5. Encourage your teen-ager to get along well with teachers and other school personnel.
6. Support school personnel in disciplinary procedures.
7. Give your youngster enough educational support.
8. Appreciate the value of co-curricular and extra curricular school activities.
9. Discourage teen-agers' joining illegal secret clubs and societies.
10. Encourage your youngster to stay in school until he completes his education.
11. Investigate the school work-study program as it pertains to your teen-ager.

SUMMARY

This chapter discussed ways in which parents can help their teen-agers derive maximum benefit from school.

The next chapter will discuss work, vocational training, and money in the lives of teen-agers and suggest ways in which parents may help youngsters find themselves vocationally, gain work experience, and use money wisely.

Chapter 11

Work and Money

"AN OCCUPATION IS part of a way of life—a big part," says Dr. Paul Brainard, psychologist and vocational guidance expert. "For most of us, work is our greatest interest next to our family. It takes up at least half our waking time. Our work and personalities constantly affect each other."

Dr. David Ausubel, research specialist at the University of Illinois, reports that in all cultures the individual's occupation, broadly conceived, is the most important factor in establishing his social status in the community and his competence in the minds of his neighbors. This image of the man is usually generalized to his family; thus the public attitudes toward a family member depend largely on the occupation of the head of the household.

Young people determine to a considerable degree the kinds of lives they will lead when they choose a vocation and prepare to go into it. It is important, therefore, that they choose a vocation that is right for them.

Most parents want to help their teen-agers get a good start occupationally and are looking for ways to do this. The suggestions that follow may be useful.

Recognize the need for vocational guidance and careful planning. A few generations ago, many boys followed in their fathers' footsteps occupationally: farmers' sons became farmers, doctors' sons became doctors, millers' sons became millers. That situation has changed. Only a small percentage of today's boys will make a living when they grow up doing what their father does. Furthermore, most parents do not want their sons to follow Dad's line of work, except those in the professions. Dr. William Dyer reported an Iowa study recently, for example, which revealed that in white-collar occupations only 24 per cent of fathers and 3 per cent of mothers want the son to enter Dad's occupation and that in blue-collar vocations, only 13 per cent of fathers and 18 per cent of mothers want the son to pursue Dad's type of work.

Confusion created by parental job dissatisfaction—as reflected in the Dyer study and others—is compounded by the vast number of occupations that exist in today's complex society. The Dictionary of Occupational Titles lists several thousand jobs. Choosing the right one is often a difficult task for a youngster.

The entrance of women into the working world has also made the vocational scene more complicated as well as more attractive. Today, more than 60 per cent of all employable women work for pay. Guidance for today's youth must include, therefore, both boys and girls.

The youngster who knows what he wants to do for a living is fortunate because he can go ahead, make plans, carry them out in school and on the job. He is not the typical teen-ager, however; he is the exception, not the rule. The average teen-ager does not know for sure what he wants to do for a living. Dr. H. H. Remmers, Director of the Purdue Opinion Panel, found in a nationwide survey that 56 per cent of the high school students wondered what kind of work they might be best suited for, 42 per cent questioned their ability to succeed at any job.

Dr. Remmers found also that many high school students expect to attain a higher occupational level than is likely or even possible. For example, more than half of all the youngsters hope to become professional persons—doctors, lawyers, ministers, engineers, etc. In reality, only 20 per cent of the adolescent population has the mental ability required for the professions, and some of these persons have neither the aptitude nor the interest necessary to achieve success in them. Furthermore, many persons who might qualify in other ways are financially unable to complete the required education and training. Probably not more than 8 per cent of the teen-age population will go into the professions.

The University of Michigan's Survey Research Center studies of adolescent boys and girls indicate clearly the expectation among teen-agers that the occupation they enter will determine their social status as well as their income. Among lower- and middle-class youngsters there is a strong desire to move up the economic and social ladders through occupations. Half of the girls interviewed were daughters of manual workers, but only 7 per cent of them wanted their husbands to hold manual jobs, and only 4 per cent chose manual jobs for themselves. The urge, apparently normal in our culture, to move upward occupationally, in social status, in personal achievement, and in living comfort makes middle-class youngsters want to become upper-class adults; similarly, it makes lower-class youngsters want to become middle-class adults.

Most teen-age boys and girls face eventual occupational disillusionment. Some of them, however, will move upward vocationally, socially, and financially. They will go farther in school than their parents, hold better jobs, make more money, buy larger cars, live in more expensive houses, enjoy greater social prestige, experience increased social acceptance. In doing so, they will fulfill their parents' ambitions, and, interestingly enough, they will probably tend—as a result—to reject their parents.

Studies of adolescents' concepts of the world of work, of themselves, and of the ingredients necessary for success on the job make it clear that most teen-agers need vocational guidance. Furthermore, they want it. Dr. Ross Mooney, whose *Problem Checklists* are widely used in schools throughout the nation, finds that vocational problems rank first, as a rule, among the various kinds of concerns about which high school students worry. Dr. Hugh M. Bell reported findings from a study conducted under auspices of the American Council on Education that two-thirds of the high school students are most seriously concerned about the achievement of economic security— an occupational problem. Dr. David Ausubel interprets this adolescent preoccupation with the vocational future as a symptom that the teen-agers' primary goals ". . . are really predicated upon his inclusion in the adult world." In other words, to the teen-ager, being employed means being grown-up.

Help your youngster secure reliable information, competent guidance, wise counseling. Dr. John Kahl says in *The American Class Structure* that ". . . the major influence of a family over a son is to shape his thinking in the direction of a certain level in the occupational hierarchy." Studies of motivation indicate clearly the very significant influence parental attitudes have on youngster's scholastic achievement and vocational aspirations. Young people usually try to become what their parents think they should become.

The Institute of Student Opinion of *Scholastic Magazine* revealed recently that teen-agers look more often to their parents than to anyone else for vocational guidance. More than 11,000 teen-agers across the nation were asked to identify the sources they would tap for helpful advice in planning their careers. Their replies and the percentages of frequency were:

"My father, mother, or other relatives"	28%
"My school guidance counselor"	18%
"My teachers"	17%
"A business or professional man"	15%
"Books, magazines, or other published material"	8%
"My minister, priest, or Sunday school teacher"	7%
"Friends about my own age"	6%
"Other"	3%

Parental responsibility for helping the teen-ager get the best possible guidance is clear. Parents may do many things in this direction. They should not try to make a youngster's choice for him, rather they should encourage him to make the right choice for himself.

Parents who are interested and adequately informed know they must find out as much as possible about their child—his abilities, aptitudes, talents, and interests—if they are to help him move in the right direction. They can learn much through observing the youngster at home and in the neighborhood, noting the things he does well, those he does poorly, and by interpreting the differences between performance and occupational aptitudes. Furthermore, they may experiment by making available interesting literature on various subjects and by providing basic, elementary vocational tools and equipment to see how he handles them, how he reacts. They can talk with him about his interests, his likes and dislikes, his vocational desires. They wisely let him do most of the talking; they listen patiently, observe him casually, carefully, looking always for the sparkle of enthusiasm in his eye and the sound of excitement in his voice that spell genuine interest. Mentally, they mark with a "plus" the activities that evoke these reactions and mark those for which he has no enthusiasm at all with a "minus." These three methods— observation, experimentation, and conversation—are available to all parents who want to help their teen-agers discover themselves vocationally.

Parents may also learn much about their teen-ager's abilities, aptitudes, talents and interests by talking with school personnel—teachers, counselors, school psychologists. Most modern secondary schools have a routinized, formal testing program that subjects teen-agers to group tests in mental maturity, academic achievement, vocational interest, and, in isolated cases, personality adjustment. These tests are usually given periodically throughout the youngster's school career, but you will be especially interested in the ones he takes in about the ninth and twelfth grades, which ordinarily include batteries specifically designed to help teen-agers choose the right vocation. The school counselor or psychologist will interpret your youngster's results in a parent conference, which you will probably have to request. The information you gain should help you guide your teen-ager to the field of work that is best for him.

School testing programs are sometimes not adequate and, in some instances, nonexistent. In any case, parents may want to have their youngster tested at a public or private vocational guidance agency. The most expensive type of study involves individual intelligence and aptitude tests (as contrasted with group tests, which are really rough screening devices). The Stanford-Binet Intelligence Test and the Wechsler Adult Intelligence Scale, the two most commonly used individual tests of mental ability, give the counselor a much more accurate, detailed picture of the individual's mental functioning than do group intelligence tests; furthermore, they may provide important clues to latent vocational strengths and weaknesses. Specific aptitudes, such as manual dexterity, visual alertness and discrimination, and auditory discriminatory skill, are measured further by individual aptitude tests, which provide significant information that is generally not available from group tests. Thus, youngsters do secure much valuable guidance information from individual studies. The money their parents spend in this venture is usually well-invested.

The information that comes from expert professional vocational advisement usually meets parents' approval. The parent is sometimes disappointed, however, that the tests do not bear out his own convictions about the teen-ager nor support his desire for the youngster's future. When this happens, the parent is wise to talk the problem over with the counselor, clarifying what he—the parent—knows about the youngster that seems incompatible with the test results. Tests are not infallible; it is always possible that the test results are wrong. The parent should also discuss the matter with the teen-ager, who is, after all, the one who should be most concerned. If the youngster does not agree with you, do not force the issue; let it rest for a while. Leave the door open so you can talk with him about it later; otherwise, if you push your point of view too hard, you may find the lines of communication between you and him sorely bruised, perhaps broken.

Recognize the values and limitations of out-of-school work experience. A successful industrialist told me recently that he learned more valuable lessons from jobs that he held while attending high school and college than he learned from classroom instruction. Many businessmen feel that previous work experience is very important for prospective employees, even if the work is menial. Punctuality, trustworthiness, and honest effort are some of the important lessons youngsters learn by working for pay.

The most common job for teen-age girls is baby-sitting, which may be done without interfering seriously with a youngster's social and educational life. The competent baby sitter is in demand during all four seasons of the year, days and evenings, school nights and weekends. A girl who is greatly in demand cannot fulfill all the requests for service she may receive. If she does a good job consistently, her services are continually in demand, and this happy situation gives her a feeling of confidence, a feeling of being wanted and needed. Baby-sitting may vary from watching television in the neighbor's home at night while the children sleep to intelligent, informed child care, which provides child-rearing experiences that should be valuable to the girl in the future when she marries and has children of her own.

Recently, two teen-age girls in our neighborhood organized an informal play group, a nursery school type of child-care service that met each weekday morning during the summer in the girls' own back yard. They solicited young children—two to four years old—as enrollees and charged their mothers a small weekly fee. They read stories to the children, taught them games, supervised their play. These girls performed a well-received neighborhood service that mothers appreciated and for which they were very willing to pay. The experience the girls gained may help them later as teachers or nurses or mothers. The service was so successful the girls plan to repeat it next summer.

Younger teen-age boys find paper delivery routes easy to obtain but difficult to service properly and well. The turnover in these jobs is high because the hours are usually difficult (early morning or early evening), the weather interferes often (rain, snow, cold), and the responsibilities are sometimes too advanced (collecting money, keeping records, etc.). Parents, being soft-hearted, may end up driving the youngster on his route to deliver papers during bad weather, to collect subscription payments after dark and at other times when they prefer that the boy not be out alone. Thus, paper delivery routes become, in some cases, better training for parents than for their offspring. Boys who do the job well on their own, however, gain a wealth of experience and make good money in the process.

Many teen-agers begin earning money by working at modest jobs in stores, by doing small but necessary tasks for neighbors—such as mowing lawns, cleaning windows, taking care of pets. Summer jobs for the fourteen- or fifteen-year-old girl include clerical, sales, and stock work in retail stores as well as domestic service such as babysitting and nurse's aid. A fifteen-year-old boy might get a summer job as a delivery boy, sales clerk, packer or stockhandler; or he might wash cars, caddy at the golf course, or work on a farm.

Sixteen- and seventeen-year-old boys and girls have many more opportunities for jobs—both full-time and part-time—than do their younger brothers and sisters. Office work, employment in restaurants and resorts, assistantships to skilled craftsmen, filling station and factory jobs beckon tens of thousands of them each summer. In many instances, teen-agers who prove themselves capable of summer jobs continue working after school and Saturdays during the school year, thereby gaining further valuable work experience and earning money as they learn.

Out-of-school work experiences offer valuable lessons in living as well as monetary rewards. The Secretary of Labor of the United States suggests the important objective of such jobs is ". . . to acquire the disciplines that apply to all employment—responsibility for conscientious effort, taking direction from a job superior, promptness, proper handling of money, and learning to work with others." Youngsters who earn money working for employers other than their parents and relatives will probably have a

distinct advantage later over those who work only for
parents and relatives or those who never work for pay.
There is something about having a real job that makes
boys and girls more serious, more mature, more self-
sufficient. A job gives them poise, makes them feel
confident and adequate. Many boys and girls pay their
own way through college or other beyond-high-school
education and training with money they earn in part-time
employment and summer jobs.

The limitations of part-time jobs and summer employment are many. The jobs consist, in most instances, of
simple tasks that require little mental effort and may
become monotonous and boring to the capable,
energetic, imaginative youngster after the novelty of the
job wears off. A variety of jobs is usually better than a
single assignment for a long period of time. Many jobs
in different fields give the youngster a wide background
of experience and relieve the monotony of simple
repetition that marks unskilled tasks.

The best job for the teen-ager may be one related
directly to the vocation that he plans to enter. The boy,
for example, who hopes to become a physician may
profit most from working as a hospital corpsman, where
he may observe doctors and nurses in action and orient
himself to the realities of the profession he intends to
enter. In some cases, the teen-ager may change his mind
as a result of his work experience, decide he does not
want that kind of life after all, for he finds neither joy
nor satisfaction in it. This, too, is an important lesson. It
is one that many persons who are vocationally
inexperienced learn too late, after they have spent many
years in college preparing themselves at great expense
for a field of work that they should not enter.

Teen-agers who work while going to school sacrifice
some social life—a situation that may be disadvantageous;
yet studies show that youngsters who are so employed get
in trouble less frequently than those who have too much
time on their hands. Employed youths spend less money
than idle ones because they have less time in which to

spend it; furthermore, the money they spend is usually their own, while idle youths must get money from their parents. The objective evidence that is available indicates convincingly that out-of-school work experiences have more advantages than disadvantages, socially and financially, for boys and girls alike.

Part-time employment and summer jobs are sometimes blamed for causing students to drop out of high school or college. Some students find themselves earning good wages—better wages, in fact, than they would probably earn by continuing school and entering a different field of work. They drop out of school, therefore, and go to work. They may get married or enter some other venture unrelated to school. They tend to limit their future earning power by doing so and risk unwittingly getting stuck in a "blind-alley" job that leads nowhere.

These youngsters would probably not make this mistake if they secured adequate school guidance and counseling before dropping out of school. Longitudinal studies reveal that boys and girls who accept competent guidance and vocational counseling in high school do not end up in "blind-alley" jobs; those who receive no guidance and counseling, however, get into jobs that lead often to little more than chronic boredom and continual dissatisfaction. Parents are wise, therefore, who encourage their teenagers to take advantage of the guidance and counseling services available to them in the school and in community agencies.

Encourage your teen-ager to participate in school work-experience education if he can profit from it. Out-of-school work experience would probably be valuable to all teenagers; yet opportunities for meaningful jobs for adolescents are steadily decreasing in number as machines and labor-saving devices take over many tasks that people previously performed. It is becoming increasingly difficult at the same time for young people to obtain employment without having had experience on a job; thus, the problem of initial entry into a vocation is becoming more troublesome.

The most promising answer to this problem is a well-planned, well-administered school work-experience education program carried out by the high school in cooperation with local businesses, industries, and community agencies. A student in such a program studies a field of work at school and works part-time in the same field in a business, industry, or agency. He receives school credit and payment ordinarily for his work. Thus, the high school commercial student attends school five hours a day, works three hours a day outside of school in . an office. His teacher supervises his work at school, his employer supervises him on the job; the two of them together evaluate his over-all performance at school and on the job.

People who have been involved in work-experience programs recognize great value in them. Students become more serious about school, do better work, behave more maturely. Teachers like the program because it brings academic work and the world of work closer together, helping bridge the gap between school and vocations. Employers like it because the students are enthusiastic, energetic, eager to learn and to please.

Employers are under no obligation whatsoever to keep work-experience students on as full-time employees after they complete high school; yet studies show that many of them do so because these youngsters work out better as full-time employees than newly hired ones who have not had this training.

Work-experience programs vary in size and complexity according to the school population and the nature of the community; the small, residential community school may have a modest program because the community employment sources are limited; the large, metropolitan school, on the other hand, can have an extensive program with the cooperation of many business and industrial leaders and community agencies. Any well-run school work-experience program is better than none, for it brings school and community closer together as well as giving youngsters practical vocational experiences.

The work-experience program in the Santa Barbara

County (California) Schools typifies a well-planned, well-coordinated program that has served as a model in several states.[1] This program, organized cooperatively by the schools, businesses, industries, and community agencies, offers three types of work-experience education: exploratory, general, and vocational. The first type, exploratory, is a program of work without pay, on school time, with school supervision and school credit, in a business, industry, or profession, to help the student discover his aptitudes and interests in a variety of work situations. Exploratory opportunities are provided in hospitals, clinics, schools, banks, lawyers' offices, laboratories, governmental agencies, and other organizations. The student moves from station to station within an organization, learning about all departments and the standards of behavior and work required by each. The second type, general, is a program of part-time employment with pay, during school hours or after school, with school supervision and school credit, in a business, industry, or profession. The student must meet the standards required by the employer and those required by the school; thus the general program is designed to give him practical experience in a real job with exacting standards and monetary reward. The third type, vocational, is a program of paid work directly related to the lifetime occupation that the student expects to enter. It presents a real-life laboratory for the student's occupational education and training. The vocational type of work-experience education is the most widely practiced in Santa Barbara County and, incidentally, throughout the nation. School personnel and employers involved in the Santa Barbara work-experience education program recently discussed the benefits that students, schools, the community, and the nation derive from such a program. Their conclusions, which follow in summary, have far-reaching

[1] The author is grateful to Dr. Esther Grace Nolan, Research and Guidance Consultant, Los Angeles County Schools, and former secretary of the California Educational Research and Guidance Association, for reporting the Santa Barbara County School's work-experience education program.

implications for teen-agers, parents, schools, and communities throughout America.

Benefits to students. Working in the adult world has given students a new feeling of belonging. Being given adult responsibilities has made students accept responsibilities in a more mature way. Young people who have tried out a variety of work situations are better able to choose the careers for which they are best suited and in which they can contribute the most as citizens. The work experience education program has brought teen-agers and adults closely together in a way that was not possible before.

Benefits to the schools. Close association of school and business, which results from work-experience education, helps schools become aware of changes in the curriculum that are necessary to prepare young people for the demands of the working world. Careful supervision of student-employees, conferences between school personnel and employers and between students and work coordinators, and careful evaluations make school personnel more aware of what boys and girls must be taught if they are to succeed on the job.

Benefits to the community. The organized, carefully planned approach to work-experience education has been received with great favor by the citizens of the community. They have seen how the young people can be relied upon for really important work. Giving them this meaningful activity has demonstrated that they are less likely to get into trouble: work-experience education suggests thereby a partial answer to the prevention of juvenile delinquency. At a Santa Barbara Town Meeting, several teen-agers who took work-experience education expressed their opinion that youth problems could be solved not by more recreation, but by an extension of work opportunities such as those they had enjoyed.

Benefits to the nation. The great need is obvious in our country today for highly skilled specialists whose education, training, and experience relate meaningfully to the great scientific and technical advances of the modern age. Young people who take work-experience education during high school and college will be better able to make important contributions to the nation when their school days are over.

Work-experience education programs are viewed by the United States Office of Education and the Department of Labor as being probably the best answer to many problems in the education and training of modern high school youth. If the high school your teen-ager attends has such a program, have him investigate it, explore the possibilities it holds to help him gain meaningful experiences in the world of work that relate to his studies at school. If, on the other hand, the school has no such program, you may want to suggest to school authorities the possibility of establishing one in the interests of youth and the wider community.

Help your youngster find full-time employment when he is ready for it. The youngster who drops out of high school enters the labor market at a very great disadvantage. He has no vocational skill, is inadequately educated, and has probably made a poor school record. He is likely to search a long time before he finds employment; he will probably drift aimlessly from one job to another. The United States Bureau of Labor Statistics reports that twice as many drop-outs are unemployed as high school graduates and that the lowest paid workers are usually drop-outs. Furthermore, high school drop-outs, being idle too much and facing bleak futures, are the ones most likely to become social delinquents. In view of these facts, the greatest favor you can do your teen-ager is to convince him he should *not* drop out but should remain in school until he has completed the education he needs to enter the world of work with the odds in his favor.

If your teen-ager drops out of school in spite of your well-intentioned advice or if he graduates from high school and wants to work rather than go to college, there are some things you may do to help him get started. *First,* remember that the final decision regarding a job is his to make, not yours; therefore, understand that you are merely trying to help him, not attempting to tell him what to do. *Second,* get informational guides for him from the public library and the state employment service. These publications tell him how to dress, how to apply for a job, how to make the best impression on prospective employers. *Third,* have him go to the local office of the state department of employment to be interviewed and to file an application for work. *Fourth,* teach him how to read the "Help Wanted" columns of the newspaper and how to decide which jobs to apply for. *Fifth,* ask your friends and neighbors for information regarding openings for which your teen-ager might qualify. *Sixth,* make a list of the community's businesses, industries, and organizations that seem likely to be employers of young, rather inexperienced persons.

Out-of-school adolescents who are idle become bored, unhappy, discouraged. If your youngster cannot find a job, perhaps he can become interested in returning to high school, in taking vocational training beyond high school, or in going on to college. (Educational Testing Service estimates that 50,000 youngsters who drop out of high school each year are good college material.) He would certainly be better off improving his chances for vocational success via school than sitting around the house or loafing in the neighborhood pool halls and bowling alleys, feeling useless.

Teach your teen-ager how to use money wisely. Young people should be taught to use money wisely whether they earn it themselves or get it as an allowance. Many parents give very young children a small allowance—ten, fifteen, twenty-five cents a week—to teach them number concepts before they start to school. Thus, some preschoolers know that a nickel is worth five pennies, that two nickels are worth a dime, that a penny will buy a stick of gum or a candy sucker, that if they buy a penny sucker with a nickel, the man will give them several pennies change. They may also accumulate a number of coins and learn, with parental help, to count them correctly.

During the middle years—between early childhood and adolescence—boys and girls who receive allowances or earn money learn much about money values, saving, spending, accounting. If permitted considerable freedom of choice within reasonable guidelines or boundaries, they usually develop a good sense of the purpose and value of money. They know, for example, that money is a means to an end, not an end in itself. They know that the numerical values of coins and currency do not change but that their purchasing values do change. They know that they should save part of their income, that they must save part of it if they are to buy the more expensive items they hope to possess. They know they must keep track of their money if it is to fit meaningfully into their personal plans. They know from personal experience that some things they buy are not worth the money they cost and that an item must be carefully evaluated, therefore, before it is purchased. They know they cannot have everything: money goes only so far; one must pick and choose before he buys. These are some of the lessons youngsters should learn about money before they reach adolescence.

Teen-agers need considerably more money than pre-adolescents because they are older, more mature. They dress more neatly, pay more attention to good grooming. They go out on their own alone or with groups to places that require money. They date. They need more commercial products. In view of these needs, most parents who give their children allowances increase the amount considerably when the youngsters become adolescents. Sizeable increases are undoubtedly in order. An alternative is to permit the teen-ager to go to work and earn money in lieu of increased allowance. Some parents do both—increase the allowance and encourage their teen-ager to add to it through earnings from part-time jobs.

Teen-agers who have had experience with their own money during early childhood and the middle years and who have learned through errors as well as successes to use money wisely are usually able to manage their increased income. They keep a record of income and expenditures. They plan ahead for important purchases and save money to make them. They lay some money aside for "a rainy day." Some of them buy a few bonds or stocks. Many boys save money to buy a car or to operate and maintain the car their parents buy for them.

Parents are wise who permit their teen-agers to spend their own .money in whatever ways they choose that are reasonable. Teen-agers should select their own clothing, for example, and pay for it themselves with their own money. This practice is much more effective than doling out money for each specific purchase and is better than having parents select the teen-ager's clothing for him. Adolescent boys and girls are trying to grow up. They should undoubtedly be permitted opportunities such as this to *act* grown-up. They will make some mistakes in judgment, especially if they have not been permitted previously to make decisions or to manage money earlier in life. They must nevertheless begin some time to assume these responsibilities themselves; adolescence is none too soon to start. The same principle holds for most other normal teen-age expenditures, such as automobile expenses, entertainment costs, and "mad money" purchases. The teen-ager must learn to decide such matters for himself and to accept the consequences of his decisions, be they good or bad.

Parents should carefully evaluate the teen-ager's needs in determining the size of an allowance. Giving a youngster too much money can do him as much harm as not giving him enough. The best approach to this problem is perhaps to sit down with the youngster, talk with him about his needs, decide the kinds of purchases he will be expected to make from his allowance and the kinds you will pay for separately—such as costs of medical and dental care, family vacation expenses, parties at home, family outings, tuition, school books and supplies. The arrangements should be mutually satisfactory to the teen-ager and the parent. This way all parties concerned will feel that the plan is fair and just.

Consider carefully the question of charge accounts for teen-agers. There is a nationwide trend among department stores to permit credit accounts to teen-agers, even to thirteen- and fourteen-year-olds. Store officials open such accounts at the youngster's request, without parental consent; parents are informed, however, and if they object, the account is closed at once. If the parents do not object, the teen-ager is permitted to buy to a stated limit—fifty dollars, for example, repayable at five dollars a month. The usual credit fee is one per cent per month on the unpaid balance—which represents approximately 18 per cent interest but barely pays the store's accounting costs.

Stores that extend credit to teen-agers insist that buying "on time" helps youngsters learn how to budget expenses, makes them recognize the importance of having credit privileges and maintaining a good credit rating, causes them to purchase wisely, forces them to pay for their own purchases rather than charging them to their parents, makes them keep their promises to pay, and teaches them to accept responsibility maturely in an age of easy credit.

I am generally opposed to credit accounts for teen-agers. Such plans teach youngsters to spend money they do not have rather than teaching them to budget their money wisely. They give teen-agers the illusion that they are getting something for nothing—until the "account payable" notice arrives. They fail to tell them about the money they could save by paying cash, thereby avoiding the service charge. They teach them nothing about the virtue of delaying a purchase until they have saved enough money to pay for it in full. They tempt them to buy things they cannot afford or do not genuinely need.

Stores that extend credit to teen-agers hope, of course, to develop steady customers while they are young. Department stores are in business to make money, not to educate adolescents—which is the job of the schools and the home. Parents must weigh this problem of teen-age credit carefully in their minds, make a decision, and stand by it.

Credit buying by adults on the huge scale that exists in America today seems generally unwise and unsound for the consumer, for the seller, for the nation's economy.[2] As for credit accounts for teen-agers, it is probably a serious mistake to encourage youngsters to spend money before they get it. There are exceptions to this rule, of course; however, they are so rare they need not concern us here.

Review of major points

1. Recognize the need for vocational guidance and careful planning.
2. Help your youngster secure reliable information, competent guidance, wise counseling.
3. Recognize the values and the limitations of out-of-school work experiences.
4. Encourage your teen-ager to participate in school work-experience education if he can profit from it.
5. Help your youngster find full-time employment when he is ready for it.
6. Teach your teen-ager how to use money wisely.
7. Consider carefully the question of charge accounts for teen-agers.

SUMMARY

This chapter discussed work, vocational training, and money in the lives of. teen-agers and suggested ways in which parents may help youngsters find themselves vocationally, gain work experience, and use money wisely.

The next chapter will discuss problems adolescents face when they expect to go to college and suggest ways in which parents can help their teen-agers plan successfully for getting a college education.

[2] For an insightful analysis of the weaknesses and dangers in widespread, loosely controlled consumer credit, see *Buy Now, Pay Later,* by Hillel Black (New York: William Morrow & Company, 1961).

Chapter 12

Preparing for College

MORE YOUNG PEOPLE go to college[1] today than ever before in our nation's history. Almost half of 1960's high school graduates went on to college, and approximately thirty per cent of all college-age Americans were in institutions of higher learning. Clarence Faust, vice-president of the Ford Foundation, predicted the same year, on the basis of a poll conducted privately by Elmo Roper & Associates, that American college and university enrollments of 1970 will be double those of 1960, thus approaching a total of seven million students.

Higher education is obviously "big business"—let there be no doubt about that. Furthermore, it is becoming everybody's business. Dr. Frank Bowles, president of the College Entrance Examination Board, predicted recently that by 1970 a college degree win be considered as essential as a high school diploma was in 1960. The question prospective employers of the future will ask applicants is not "Do you have a high school diploma?" but "Where did you go to college?" and "Did you graduate?" Persons who cannot reply positively to these questions will probably find employment increasingly difficult to obtain.

The Ford Foundation survey by Roper and Associates found that most American parents want their children to go to college, but not many of them are prepared to meet the cost. Almost seven out of ten parents interviewed in five thousand families said they expect to send their children to college; yet sixty per cent of the parents who expect to send their youngsters to college had no savings plan specifically for that purpose. They said, furthermore, that they expect college costs to remain about the same

[1] The term *college* as used in this chapter refers to accredited colleges, universities, graduate schools, community colleges, junior colleges. It does not include trade schools or business training schools—sometimes called "colleges"—which are not accredited as colleges by recognized accrediting associations.

across the years, revealing thereby their illusion that educational expenses are divorced from the nation's economy, which is actually marked with inflation, periodic recessions, and occasional depressions. Mr. Faust, interpreting the survey results, says, "American parents apparently need to know more about the economics of higher education and to adopt a more systematic approach to college savings. In the lifetime of the typical American family, the outlay for college and the buying of a home are the two largest investment expenditures."

The financial factor in going to college is undoubtedly an important one. It is only one of several factors, however, that parents must consider if they are to face the matter squarely and meet it realistically. The suggestions that follow may help parents in this task.

Realize that college is not for everyone. Almost half of today's high school graduates go on to an institution of higher learning; yet only about sixty per cent of these young people stay to complete their studies. Most college students who drop out do so because they make failing grades or because they do not want to continue. Some of them quit because they do not have enough money; others, however, who have little or no money stay in college through their own efforts or with temporary outside aid. Most college drop-outs seem probably to have been inappropriate candidates in the first place. One might conclude justifiably, therefore, that perhaps forty per cent of all the youngsters who go on from high school to college probably should not go; they would be better candidates for nonacademic education and training or for immediate full-time employment.

College is appropriate not only for 60 per cent of the young men and women who enroll but also, strangely enough, for a very large number of youngsters who do not try to enroll. The boys and girls who are not in college but should be there are rapid learners, have superior minds and better-than-average talents; yet they look upon college as an elusive dream, something quite unattainable. Nation-wide test surveys show that only one-third of the nation's brightest boys—that is, those in the topmost 20 per cent of the total population in terms of mental ability—graduate from college; two-thirds of them drop out or do not enter college in the first place! Educators and federal manpower experts agree that this loss of prospective students with outstanding mental abilities represents one of the greatest, most dramatic wastes in our nation today. They urge parents and teachers to encourage these youngsters to go to college; they are trying also to establish adequate financial aid to needy students with superior abilities.

Parents who recognize their children's superior aptitudes for scholastic achievement early in life and who encourage them to go to college do them a very great favor. Parents who discourage superior youngsters from going to college because they cannot afford it do them a very great injustice. Today the individual who has superior ability should be urged to move ahead educationally *regardless of his financial status;* the nation needs talented, gifted young people; there is financial aid for the needy, gifted youngster if he will but seek it out. More will be said about this later in this chapter.

Parents who have a child with less-than-college-level ability should accept him as he is and help him prepare for a less-than-college-level goal that he can attain with his limited ability. Few experiences are more frustrating for a child or an adolescent than being expected to achieve far above his ability to achieve. "I'm dumb," the youngster tells the high school counselor. "Mom and Dad want me to go to college like they did and be a big success. But I don't have what it takes. I study all the time. I try real hard. But I don't get good grades no matter how hard I try. Like I said, I'm just dumb."

The youngster may not be as "dumb" as he thinks; he is probably overly critical of himself and regards himself as a failure because in his parents' minds he is a failure—and he knows it. He is probably among the 50 or 60 per cent of the high school students who should not go to college. He would probably be successful in non-academic education and training and should prepare to enter a trade or some other vocational field that does not require a college education.

Parents are wise who recognize non-college aptitudes in their children and accept them. There is no disgrace in having a child who is not college material. It is a great mistake, however, to try to remold him into a candidate for higher education.

Neither is it a mark of personal glory to have a superior child, since the gift of superior intelligence is an act of God. It would seem disgraceful, however, to suggest that such a child not go on to college, that he should do nothing worthwhile with his unusual abilities.

Identify your youngster's mental abilities as early as possible. Ways of identifying young people's mental abilities were discussed on pages 133-137 and need not be repeated here. The suggestion was made that parents who are in doubt about their child's mental ability should discuss it with school personnel and, if still in doubt, should have their youngster evaluated by a professional psychologist who is qualified to administer, score, and interpret tests of mental ability and emotional stability. This suggestion was made with reference to high school students because they were the subject of discussion in that chapter. The problem can usually be cleared up long before high school if the parents seek help from a competent psychologist, who can usually identify with individual tests the general level of mental ability of a very young child, especially when he is either unusually intelligent or mentally retarded. A few years later, when the child has completed three or four years of formal schooling, another individual psychological evaluation is generally regarded as being the most accurate measure of the youngster's prospects for future academic success in high school and college. It is not possible, of course, to predict a youngster's future performance with unerring accuracy because tests are not infallible, and intelligence is only one of several factors involved in college success. Nevertheless, a valid measure of your child's mental abilities should be very valuable to you as an aid to regarding him objectively and planning his educational future wisely.

Recognize how your attitudes influence your youngster's desire to be successful in college. The desire to go to college is not inborn, nor does it come about as a matter of course; it must be instilled. Boys and girls tend to adopt their parents' attitudes toward most things in life, including those concerning college. Parents who are genuinely interested in scholarship and academic achievement transmit this interest as a rule to their youngsters. Parents who, on the other hand, consider scholarship a pastime for "egg-heads," academic talent a sign of physical weakness, and school achievement a waste of time convey these unfortunate attitudes to their children. These parents are usually poorly educated and suffer an unenviable socio-economic position. They insist that college is not for "the likes of us." Their hopeless, disparaging, negative attitude discourages their children and accounts unquestionably for many mentally superior youngsters' refusal to go to college.

Dr. Ralph Tyler's researches in motivation suggest that parental aspirations for occupational and academic achievement are conveyed to the child during the first ten years of his life and are not markedly modified later by school or community. This does not mean, however, that parents and teachers should do nothing thereafter. On the contrary, parents should reinforce their positive feelings about higher education continually throughout the youngster's junior high and senior high school years. The importance of this principle is illustrated by the recent Harvard study, which revealed that 89 per cent of the youngsters whose parents advocated college went to college, while only 27 per cent of the adolescents whose parents were disinterested about college enrolled in spite of their parents' passive attitudes.

Some boys and girls whose parents are indifferent toward college are encouraged by their teachers to go on to an institution of higher learning. Teachers recognize underprivileged, mentally gifted children who are often ignored by their parents, and they help them get scholarships or student-aid loans. Ministers, youth leaders, and insightful relatives recognize exceptional abilities too and lend encouragement and moral support. Dr. E. O. Swanson found, for example, through personal interviews that men who twenty years earlier had been superior high school students and who went to college gave credit for their decision to "personal encouragement" by a relative (including parents), a teacher, a minister, or a friend. The other men, who were equally superior in high school but did not go to college, said they could not recall anyone having ever suggested that they go to college.

If no adult cares, the youngster does not care. It is often as simple as that!

Help your youngster plan for college long before it is time to attend. It is advisable to start planning for college long before a teen-ager completes high school. If a student waits until his senior year to start planning for college, he is fortunate if he does not encounter much frustration and disappointment. He will probably find most college enrollment quotas filled and the institutions' doors closed to new applicants.

The American School Counselors Association suggests that parents whose child shows potential for college success should start laying plans no later than when the youngster is in the eighth grade. At this time, the parents should visit the school counselor, discuss the youngster's elementary and junior high school record and the results of the standardized mental ability and academic achievement tests he has taken that would probably indicate whether he has college-level ability. If the records are encouraging, the parents and the counselor should help the student plan his ninth grade program carefully to include the science, mathematics, and language courses that are recommended as being preparatory to college.

Parents should provide an atmosphere at home that is conducive to study and an environment that encourages good study habits. The youngster should be encouraged to read extensively since reading speed and comprehension play an important role in college success.

In the ninth grade, the student should get acquainted with college catalogs, learn how to read and interpret them. The high school library and the counselor's office have college catalogs; also, any college will send its catalog to a parent or prospective student on request.

Careful study of college catalogs provides valuable information and guidance, especially when the teen-ager knows the major field in which he wants to study. His high school counselor can help him and his parents plan the rest of his high school program in line with future college study plans. The student's co-curricular activities and his personal interests outside of school can be intelligently directed to contribute to knowledge and understanding of his future field of study. Parents can contribute in this direction by providing books and equipment for home use in the teen-ager's chosen field that go beyond those available in high school and by encouraging him to use them in his spare time. This approach to learning helps the teen-ager see the meaning of college before he gets there, encourages scholastic achievement beyond school, and builds a fund of knowledge. All of these factors are important in making him a good prospect for college.

In the tenth grade, the student should be encouraged to continue studying college catalogs, especially the sections on entrance requirements. He should select one or more extracurricular activities, which need not necessarily have any relation to his proposed college plans but which should give him maximum pleasure and enjoyment. The student should seek further guidance from his counselor throughout the year whenever he needs it.

In the eleventh grade, the student should attend college information conferences and visit the college or colleges he hopes to attend. Plans should be made beforehand for him to talk with the college admissions counselor, who will consider his plans, hopes, aspirations and will explain how he might fit into the college scene if he becomes a student there. The personal interview with the admissions counselor brings to life many of the facts that appear cold in print in the college catalog; furthermore, it makes the teen-ager feel that the college is made up of people who are genuinely interested in him.

The eleventh grader should take the usual group tests at his high school and whatever aptitude and vocational interest tests his counselor recommends. He should also take the Preliminary Scholastic Aptitude Test (PSAT), a nationwide test given in October of each year for college-bound juniors. The test scores, which are reported to the students' high schools in December, correlate closely with scores on the Scholastic Aptitude Test, which the youngster takes later for college entrance. Thus, the high school junior's performance on the PSAT is usually indicative of his future performance on the college entrance examination. Students who find deficiencies in their funds of knowledge as revealed by the PSAT can take steps to make up those deficiencies, which might otherwise keep them out of the college of their choice.

In the twelfth grade, the teen-ager files application for admission to the college or colleges he wants to attend. This step is more complicated than it might seem; it usually requires the parents' help. The student also should take the Scholastic Aptitude Test, the test profile of which is accepted by approximately four hundred leading colleges and universities as one of the primary bases for student selection.

Be sure the college your teen-ager decides to attend is appropriate to his needs and abilities. There were almost 2,000 colleges in the United States in 1960, and the number continues to increase each year. To start searching for the right college without any previous knowledge of institutions of higher learning would seem a hopeless task.

Teen-agers know something ordinarily about a few colleges; they have definite—albeit often unreliable—ideas about them. For example, a student says he wants to go to

Harvard—or Yale, Stanford, Notre Dame, Purdue, Vassar, or some other well-known institution. The counselor asks, "Why this particular school?" He may receive such answers as these: "My father went there. I want to go there too." "Auntie Jane thinks it is the greatest. She wanted to go there when she was a girl, but she got married instead." "Mr. Jones, our next door neighbor, is an engineer. He went to M. I. T. He says it's the best engineering school in the country. I want to be an engineer, so I think I'll go to M. I. T." "Mr. Smith, my chemistry teacher, thinks I show great promise in science. He says he can help me get a scholarship to Tech if I want to go there. That's where he went to college." "I don't know why I want to go to Poly except I've heard a lot about it. They have a good football team. I'd like to be on a winning team, especially if I'm going to play 'pro' ball later." "My mother was an Alpha Phi on campus. She wants me to have as much fun as she had. She would simply die if I went to a different college."

Colleges differ greatly in many ways. The college your youngster chooses should fit his needs in several respects. First, it must provide the major course of study he wishes to pursue. Second, it should be outstanding in his major field of study and enjoy a reputation for producing excellent graduates who become successful later. Third, its religious philosophy should be compatible with the youngster's religious convictions, especially if he has strong ones. Fourth, the college should fit his personal preferences for coeducation or segregation of the sexes, as the case may be. Fifth, the social life at the college should be compatible with the student's personality and his reasons for being there. Sixth, the college should be accredited by the graduate divisions of major universities. This requirement is imperative if the youngster expects ever to continue his studies beyond college into higher levels of academic or professional training. Seventh, if he expects to earn a professional degree—in law, for example, or medicine— he may be wise to take his undergraduate work in a university that has a graduate school in his chosen field, since candidates for graduate school who are alumni of the university are often given preference over alumni of other institutions who have similar undergraduate records. Eighth, scholarships, tuition loans, and part-time employment should be available through the college if the student must have them to stay in school. Ninth, the distance between home and college must be satisfactory to the student. Some young people want to be near home, while others want to be far away. There is no ideal or recommended distance; it is a matter of choice that should be left up to the student. In my opinion, it is usually wise for young people to attend college a considerable distance from home so they will be on their own rather than depending on their parents as they did in high school. They mature more rapidly this way than when they live at home while attending college or live on campus and go home on weekends. Tenth, the college must be one that the student can afford financially. This requirement is not easy to determine, since private colleges with high tuition fees have more opportunities for student employment and student loans, as a rule, than do state colleges and other low-cost institutions, where competition for jobs and loans is much more intense. Eleventh, the institution should be one the youngster genuinely wants to attend. The choice should be his, not his father's nor his mother's, not his Uncle Henry's nor his Aunt Sarah's. He is the one who must live his life. He is the one who should make the final choice. To make this choice intelligently, however, he will probably need careful guidance and counseling in high school and should be continually encouraged to get it.

Help your teen-ager file applications for admission to college. The high school student should ordinarily file application for admission to a college well ahead of the time he hopes to enroll. Many colleges now are encouraging students to apply at the end of their junior year in high school, which is approximately sixteen months before they would normally be entering college. These institutions render a decision early so the student knows soon whether he will be admitted after he completes high school satisfactorily. A few colleges ask for "preliminary applications'* during the student's junior year in high school and make tentative judgments that help guide the student. Most private colleges and universities, however, accept applications for admission from high school seniors during the fall semester only—that is, from September through January or early February. A late applicant has only an outside chance of being accepted.

An application is considered to be "strong" when certain qualifications, such as those that follow, are met. (a) The student's high school marks must be acceptable according to established college standards, which vary among institutions. The most reputable schools require better than a B average; some of them require almost an A average. Other schools have lower admission standards in this respect, (b) The student must have taken certain courses in high school, most of which are academic in nature, including the following: at least two years of mathematics; two years of a foreign language; two or more years of science; social studies; and three years of English, (c) The student should rank high academically among his high school classmates, (d) He should make commendable scores on the College Entrance Examination Board Tests, (e) He should have favorable recommendations by his teachers, counselor, school principal, and community leaders, (f) He should demonstrate in his personal biographical data that he knows what he wants from college and is able to express his desires on paper in readable, well-constructed English, (g) He should present evidence of having participated actively in high school co-curricular and extracurricular activities.

Applications for admission to college are usually difficult and tedious to complete; therefore, whatever assistance you may give your youngster in completing them will be time well spent.

High school students should limit the number of applications for college admission to a reasonable number. Institutions of higher learning are asking high school counselors and administrators to urge students to refrain from filing admission applications widely and promiscuously to many colleges, a common practice by youngsters who think they may not be accepted by the college of their choice. Dr. Clyde Vroman, Director of Admissions at the University of Michigan, says, "Probably no problem is more baffling in college admissions than multiple applications. Most college-bound students submit applications generally to more than one college, the average being three to five applications for each student. Some of them, however, submit applications to twenty colleges or more. Too many students send applications for admission to colleges before finding out whether the colleges have what they want, what their chances are of being admitted, the costs of attending, and whether they would enroll in them if they were admitted." Dr. Vroman recommends strongly that students and their parents consider such matters as these before they file any applications and that they keep the number of applications at a reasonable minimum. Furthermore, the student should formally withdraw his application when he decides against enrolling in a college that has accepted him; otherwise, the college's list of prospective students is erroneous and misleading through no fault of the college but because the youngster is not thoughtful and considerate.

Face realistically the financial problems involved in getting a college education. It costs a lot of money to go to college and stay there long enough to graduate. Naturally, the costs vary greatly among the institutions according to several factors. Private institutions cost more generally than state schools, for example, because they receive no public funds (tax money) but must rely on private gifts, contributions, and tuition fees from students. Residence colleges cost more ordinarily than nonresidence schools because they are more expensive to operate and maintain. Such factors as these make it difficult to discuss college costs in specific terms rather than general ones.

Parents pay generally about 60 per cent of the costs the average American college undergraduate incurs, and scholarships and student earnings account for most of the remaining 40 per cent, according to a recent nationwide survey conducted by the University of Michigan. Investigators in this survey interviewed 2,700 families across the nation, found that many parents whose children attended college experienced considerable difficulty financially. In planning for college education for their younger children, 80 per cent of the parents expected their youngster to help pay his way with a part-time or summer job, and 10 per cent expected financial aid from scholarships, gifts, or inheritances.

Most parents have neither a definite idea of college costs nor a savings plan for this purpose, according to the Roper poll for the Ford Foundation, cited early in this chapter. To finance the children's college education at some future date, 67 per cent of the parents said they would use some form of savings or insurance; 41 per cent expect their youngsters to receive scholarships; 29 per cent expect to use current income when the time arrives; 28 per cent expect the student to earn his way; and 15 per cent expect him to apply for loans from the college or from the government.

Sixty-three of every hundred high school students in America expect to go on to college, but only twenty-two of them definitely have enough money on hand to go, according to the 1961 Institute of Student Opinion, sponsored by *Scholastic Magazine.* In a study of more than 7,000 secondary school students throughout the United States, the Institute found that approximately 65 per cent of the students who expect to go on to college are sure they will *not* have enough money or are uncertain about it. Of those who evidently will need some outside financial aid, about 80 per cent intend to work part-time and during the summer to help meet the costs; 24 per cent expect to get scholarships; 8 per cent expect to get college loans; approximately 25 per cent do not know how they will raise enough money.

There are three main ways to finance a college education: parental support, self-support, and outside support such as scholarships and loans. These ways may serve as guidelines to parents and teen-agers.

Typically, parents provide about 50 per cent of a teen-ager's college expenses; the teen-ager himself pays about 25 per cent from earnings and savings; scholarships and grants-in-aid account for 10 to 20 per cent; loans and other sources round out the remainder, according to the College Scholarship Service of the College Entrance Examination Board.

Most parents have only a hazy notion of college costs, the CEEB declares, and should talk with their teen-ager's high school counselor, ask him to estimate and analyze the costs for the first year at least.

Teen-agers who are serious about college and who genuinely want to complete their education should work during the summer and save money to help pay their costs for the subsequent school year. Many of them can also work part-time during the school year, either on campus or off, probably in the college community. There are many part-time jobs for college students: waiting tables in dining halls and restaurants, working in libraries, assisting in private and parochial schools, domestic service, and many others. Most of these jobs pay cash wages; some of them pay room and board. They all help students put themselves through college.

Student loans at low rates of interest—one to four per cent—provide another important resource upon which a needy college student may draw. This is one form of teenage credit I heartily approve. Such loans make it possible for a youngster to stay in college, complete his education, get started in his vocation or profession, pay back the loan over a period of time. This type of credit represents the student's investment in himself. In effect it raises his potential earning power by enabling him to complete his education and move into a higher occupational bracket.

Private institutions pioneered loans for needy students and still provide them. In addition, almost a dozen states have recently established government loan programs for students who are legal residents of the state. Commercial banks, insurance companies, and finance corporations are also making loans for educational expenses. The largest program, however, is the federal government's National

Defense Student Loan Program. By 1961, almost all the colleges and universities in the nation were participating in this program, which had lent many millions of dollars to full-time enrolled students. These loans, made under the National Defense Education Act, are awarded on the basis of financial need, and repayment does not begin until the student completes his education and military service.

Scholarships are popular sources of funds but are hard to get because the competition for them is intense. They were awarded primarily as prizes in years past, but now they are increasingly directed to needy bright students who would probably not be able to go to college without them. Many of them are given in combination with offers of part-time employment and/or long-term student loans. Business and industrial firms, clubs, states, foundations, religious organizations, civic groups, cultural institutions and others provide scholarships and other forms of financial assistance to needy, deserving college men and women.

Parents must ordinarily file a confidential statement of their financial status when their son or daughter is being considered for a scholarship. This statement, which is more personal, more exacting, and perhaps more exasperating than the annual Internal Revenue Service forms, probably discourages some parents from supporting the youngster's application. However, the purpose of the declaration of financial status is to make sure that the applicant really needs the money more than other individuals who are equally eager to get it. If the statement is an official one for the College Scholarship Service of the CEEB, it is filed and kept confidential, a copy being transmitted only to the official representative of the colleges and non-college sponsors of scholarships whom the parents have named to receive it.

If your teen-ager knows which college he will attend and if he does not have adequate financial support, he or you may write that institution for information and directions regarding scholarships, loans, part-time work, and summer employment.

If your youngster has not yet been accepted by a college

or has not committed himself to enter one, he should discuss these matters with his high school counselor, who probably has on hand the information the youngster needs. The counselor may in any case suggest certain library books as outside reading, some of the most important ones are:

Bowles, Frank H., *How to Get into College.* New York: E. P. Dutton and Co., 1960

Fine, Benjamin, *How to be Accepted by the College of Your Choice.* Great Neck, N.Y.: Channel Press, 1957. Paperback reprint, revised, by Popular Library, 1960

Karl, S. Donald, and Weidenfeld, Barbara Diehl, editors, *The College Handbook* (latest edition). New York: College Entrance Examination Board

Lovejoy, Clarence E., *Love joy's College Guide* (latest edition). New York: Simon and Schuster

Review of major points

1. Realize that college is not for everyone.
2. Identify your youngster's mental abilities as early as possible.
3. Recognize how your attitudes influence your youngster's desire to be successful in college.
4. Help your teen-ager plan for college long before it is time to attend.
5. Be sure the college your teen-ager decides to attend is appropriate to his needs and abilities.
6. Help your teen-ager file applications for admission to college.
7. Face realistically the financial problems involved in getting a college education.

SUMMARY

This chapter discussed some of the problems teen-agers face as they look forward to going to college and suggested ways in which parents may help them prepare.

The next chapter will discuss moral and spiritual values of adolescents and will suggest ways in which parents can help youngsters build sound ones into their lives.

Chapter 13

Moral and Spiritual Values

GROWING UP DURING adolescence involves not only growing physically and adjusting emotionally to bodily changes but implies various shifts in personality organization that affect the teen-ager's moral and spiritual values and his behavior.

The terms *values, morality,* and *spirituality* are often used loosely without clear reference to their meaning. In this discussion, however, their meanings are quite specific. Value refers to the way one feels about an idea, a concept, a belief, an ideal, a person, a place, a thing. For example, John thinks everyone should be honest; for him, honesty is, therefore, an important value. Morality refers to the appropriateness of human behavior. For instance, John values honesty as an important virtue; he thinks he is being moral, therefore, when he behaves honestly, immoral when he behaves dishonestly. Spirituality refers to one's feelings about God. To illustrate, John feels God is important in his daily life; to him, God has great value.

Adolescence tests a youngster's emotional stability and challenges the validity of his moral and spiritual values. Conscientious parents want to help teen-agers meet these tests and challenges successfully and move forward to adulthood with renewed moral courage and increased spiritual strength. The suggestions that follow may be useful in this task.

Understand the developmental changes that occur normally during adolescence. Parents start teaching moral and spiritual values to their children usually during infancy and implant them rather securely during the first five years of life.[1] They reinforce these values during the middle

[1] For a detailed discussion of this practice and ways to accomplish it effectively, see *How To Give Your Child A Good Start in Life,* by Leland E. Glover (New York: Collier Books, 1961), Chapter 11, "Establishing Religious Feelings and Moral Fibre."

years of childhood in several ways: by rewarding the youngsters for behavior that the parents approve, by punishing them for behavior that they disapprove, by encouraging them to get along with others, by teaching them to respect the rights and privileges of others, by telling them more about God, by taking them to church or to the synagogue for religious services, and many others. Parents hope the moral and spiritual values they instill in their offspring will remain intact during adolescence and throughout their lives.

Studies show that adolescence does not substantially change a youngster's moral and spiritual values; rather this stage of development causes the individual to take a closer look at his values, to analyze them, to evaluate them in the light of his new knowledge of himself and the world. Teen-agers are often reclusive, thoughtful, meditative; they examine their beliefs, wonder where they got them, wonder whether they are valid. They test mentally the values they have previously taken for granted, evaluate their own behavior against them, become more aware of morality in their thoughts and conduct. Thus they *internalize* the moral values they have long possessed, recognize the obligation to try to live up to the ideals their values imply. This process means development of conscience, which attribute is necessary to the establishment of a moral being.

The teen-ager who understands his values and lives in harmony with them feels good about himself. The youngster who thinks or behaves, on the other hand, in ways that are in conflict with his values suffers feelings of guilt, self-disgust, self-contempt, remorse. Guilt is painful; the teen-ager tries usually to avoid it. The only way he can do this successfully is "to live up to his ideals"—that is, to behave only in ways that are in accord with his real values.

The adolescent is normally less dependent than the pre-adolescent on his parents' dictates regarding morality, tending instead to establish his own criteria for judging behavior. Studies show the teen-ager is more liberal, more tolerant, more flexible than the preadolescent; thus he is likely to accept or at least tolerate behavior that he previously rejected: smoking, drinking, card playing, gambling. This does not mean, however, that he rejects his own values; on the contrary, he retains them and, feeling secure in them, can therefore accept others' behavior even when it is contrary to his own values. In reality, the teen-ager's basic values change very little in form or content from the original values established during infancy and early childhood.

Appreciate the adolescent's need to discover his moral and spiritual self. The teen-ager liberates himself gradually from slavish conformity to parental standards and gropes for other standards to replace them. He looks usually for rules, regulations, guidelines, boundaries; he finds them sometimes, but often he does not. In his confusion he may adopt slogans as easy explanations of and justification for behavior rather than seeking sound, mature answers: "You're only young once." "Here today, gone tomorrow." "Life goes on." "Crime does not pay." "Honesty is the best policy." "Big mouth, little mind." "Still waters run deep." "You can't take it with you." "You have to live." "If at first you don't succeed, try, try again." "Don't give up the ship." "Quitters don't win; winners don't quit."

Studies suggest that teen-agers like to be stimulated intellectually and challenged to think, to analyze, to search for reasons, for plausible explanations of human behavior. "Most young people seem to be eager to respond to moral values," say Drs. Robert Havighurst and Hilda Taba in *Adolescent Character and Personality.* "Even those who rebel against their environment seem to cherish an inward ideal of desirable conduct." Havighurst and Taba believe that adolescents who rebel openly and misbehave do not often reject their moral values; rather, they simply behave in ways that are contrary to their real values. They usually feel guilt-ridden as a result.

Teen-agers need desperately to discover themselves, to direct their behavior into patterns that are socially approved and in accord with their own values. Parents are wise who recognize this need and help their youngsters find themselves.

Recognize the peer group's power to influence behavior and its inability to change values. The peer group replaces parents ordinarily as the adolescent's outside behavior determinant. The peer group demands conformity to a new set of values, which are determined not by parents but by the youngsters themselves. The group is usually a very powerful enforcer of conformity to group standards, even when the standards conflict with the member's personal values. Thus, the teen-ager may behave differently as a member of a peer group than he would behave in a similar situation as an independent, self-directing individual. This discrepancy implies that expediency is the main reason the teen-ager behaves according to group standards when in the group rather than according to his own values. He goes along with the group to maintain his identity with it; yet he retains his moral values and lives by them when he is not in the group.[2]

Peer group behaviors are often troublesome to parents and teen-agers because they are frequently in conflict with values taught at home. A youngster may value neatness, for example, as a result of parental training; yet he wears sloppy, ill-fitting clothes in conformity with the peer group's mode of dress. Likewise, the youngster who values trustworthiness as a virtue may fail to keep a promise to his parents because to do so would violate a promise to the group. Thus, the peer group becomes a source of mental conflict in the teen-ager, arouses guilt feelings that lead often to self-condemnation and remorse. It continues to do this as long as it elicits behavior that is not compatible with the teen-ager's values. This type of mental conflict is usually inevitable and should be recognized by the parent as a frequent cause of moodiness and restlessness in the teen-ager at home.

Understand the traditional values of adolescent society.

---

[2] Many adults duplicate the adolescent peer group conformity pattern when, for example, they "go along with the crowd"; do something "to be a good sport"; misbehave to prove that they are not "stuffed shirts" or "wet blankets." Yet they, too, retain their basic values, keep them carefully intact.

Studies show that teen-agers and adults value generally the same virtues: honesty, integrity, friendliness, sincerity, fair-mindedness, fair play, courage, loyalty, responsibility, and many others. The differences between the values of teen-agers and those of adults are mainly matters of degree and emphasis. It is important, nevertheless, that parents understand teen-agers' feelings and their need to conform to peer group expectations. Friendliness, honesty, responsibility, and loyalty illustrate this point.

Friendliness. Teen-agers value highly the traditional virtue of friendliness, which emphasizes amiability, popularity, politeness, willingness to do favors for others, and having many friends. The teen-ager who smiles a lot, speaks kindly to others, uses good manners in interpersonal relations is usually highly accepted by his peers. The teen-age girl who is quite friendly and very attractive physically is likely to be "popular" and regarded generally as a prospective candidate for a school "queen" contest. The snobbish girl, in contrast, has trouble in her relations with her peers even if she is beautiful; snobbishness means unfriendliness, which constitutes an unforgivable sin among teen-agers.

Conflict between value and conduct arises when a youngster is obliged to act friendly when he does not feel genuinely friendly. Etiquette dictates that he must conceal his unfriendly feelings toward his peers, suppress them, or compromise them; he must act cheerful and polite if he is to be popular. Thus, regardless of his deeper feelings, the youngster who is always friendly, cheerful, good-natured, optimistic is usually regarded warmly, while the one who is unfriendly, grouchy, pessimistic, foul-tempered is generally considered a "square."

Honesty. Honesty is highly valued as a virtue by most teen-agers. The youngster who is always scrupulous in money matters, for example, is respected and credited usually with possessing personal integrity. Likewise, the youngster who always tells the truth regardless of the consequences is considered honest and is generally admired. Dishonesty is generally condemned in the teen-age culture, especially when it is practiced by an individual independent of the peer group. Cheating in school provides a good example. Cheating occurs most commonly when the teen-ager thinks he is expected to perform better than he is able to perform—due to lack of ability, lack of preparation, or some other reason. A youngster is also more likely to cheat when he feels that to perform below expectancy would disappoint the parent (or some other person to whom he looks for love and respect) and would therefore bring disapproval. Teen-agers are not often interested in the cheater's motives, even when they seem to a psychologist to be obvious and perhaps justified under the circumstances. They condemn the individual because cheating is not honest.

The situation is different, however, with reference to the peer group, which may be deliberately dishonest for a purpose. Conflict between value and conduct arises when a teen-ager feels he must behave dishonestly, against his own values, to meet the standards of the peer group. Cheating in school in this instance involves the entire group, which cheats as one. This peer group approach makes cheating seem more acceptable and less dishonest than cheating in isolation as an individual. In fact, teen-agers may regard any member of the group who does not cheat as being a "square," an "outsider," a "nonconformist." They seem to forget that cheating is dishonest and morally wrong in this situation.

Responsibility. Responsibility is a virtue that adolescents value highly, according to studies by Havighurst and Taba. This value is apparent in the deep feelings of duty a youngster feels toward self, school, home, and future vocation.

The American teen-ager feels ordinarily that his primary duty is toward his own success whether in earning grades, preparing for a vocation, or making money. This typically American concept of first duty to self contrasts sharply with the totalitarian concept of primary responsibility to the State, a value which is religiously instilled in youngsters who live under a dictatorship.

The sense of responsibility that parents instill during

early childhood and the middle years continues through adolescence, shifting gradually and in varying degrees from the home to the peer group, the school, and the wider community. Parents are wise who recognize that this re-orientation process is normal and accept it rather than criticize the teen-ager for losing interest in his traditional childhood responsibilities at home.

Loyalty. American teen-agers value loyalty but with reservations. They are generally confused about loyalty as a virtue probably because they are themselves redefining old loyalties (to parents, other authority figures, childhood friends) and are formulating new ones (to peer groups, the school, the wider community).

Reduction of loyalty to parents accompanies, as a rule, increase of loyalty to peers. Yet studies indicate that if a good parent-child relationship exists, the teen-ager's loyalty to parents remains dominant over loyalty to peers when a crisis forces him to choose between the two. This happy outcome depends, of course, upon a previous history of loyalty to parents. In cases where such loyalty did not exist prior to adolescence the chances for its being newly developed during the "teen" years are usually negligible. In other words, parents who have not inspired loyalty in their children prior to adolescence will probably never inspire it in them. Teen-agers in such cases reject their parents in the same manner that they themselves were rejected by the parents. They devote their feelings of loyalty, if any, to other persons, groups, institutions, or ideas—any of which may be either good or bad, constructive or destructive, socially acceptable or unacceptable.

Teen-agers need desperately to enjoy deep feelings of loyalty. The wise parent recognizes this need, cultivates loyalty to parents in the young child, guides the teen-ager's ever-widening loyalties to persons and institutions that are genuinely worthwhile and deserving of the youngster's loyalty.

Understand the inconsistencies among the teen-ager's moral knowledge, actual moral beliefs, stated beliefs, and conduct. The material presented thus far in this discussion suggests that teen-agers do not always behave in accordance with their actual values nor with their intellectual understanding of morality. Studies show in addition that teen-agers' knowledge of morals does not correlate highly with their moral conduct.

An adolescent's actual moral beliefs are undoubtedly the truest indicator of his character; they are difficult to measure, however, because the youngster may not be aware of them. Furthermore, if he is aware of them, he may deliberately conceal them when he thinks they are not acceptable to others. For example, the youngster who values atheism may pretend that he values religion when he is with religious friends. If they act out religious feelings (recite prayers as a group, for example), he may actually join them, do as they do, pretend to be sincere. If asked about his religious beliefs, he may lie and say he believes as the others believe. Thus, this teen-ager's conduct and stated beliefs agree, but both are incompatible with his actual beliefs. He is not in fact religious; he goes through the motions of being religious to avoid social disapproval. He compromises his actual beliefs temporarily to expedite his social relationships.

This pattern of inconsistency among knowledge, beliefs, stated beliefs, and conduct applies often not only to friendship, honesty, responsibility, and loyalty—as we have already seen—but also to moral courage, abstinence from alcohol, abstinence from tobacco, church attendance, sexual behavior prior to marriage, and many other areas of behavior.

Conduct may be inconsistent with knowledge, actual beliefs, and stated beliefs not only for expediency but for many additional reasons: duress, dictates of the culture, unusual or extenuating circumstances, inability of the youngster to generalize his actual belief to conduct accurately and with understanding—especially in the case of the dull-normal or mentally retarded youngster, the emotionally disturbed, the neurologically handicapped. Furthermore, conduct may be incompatible with the stated belief and yet in accord with a nonverbalized actual belief. For example, the teen-ager who as a young child was taught inadvertently to steal under the tutelage of dishonest parents or other adults may agree readily that it is wrong to steal. Yet he may steal in spite of his stated belief, because the stealing habit is engrained deeply in his character.

Parents are wise who realize that teen-agers do not always live up to their actual values and should not be expected to do so. Yet parents should encourage youngsters to keep their values always uppermost in their minds as guideposts to conduct, as "lighthouses" that help them emerge from darkness, confusion, dangerous situations onto the path that leads to safe harbor.

Appreciate the value of religion in the life of the teen-ager. Religious feeling is usually instilled initially in the home during infancy and early childhood and is enriched and reinforced by the church. Religious feeling is not entirely dependent, therefore, upon church attendance. Studies show rather convincingly that depth of religious feeling and frequency of church attendance do not correlate highly; that is, teen-agers who are deeply religious do not ordinarily attend church more frequently than teenagers who are not deeply religious. This does not mean, of course, that church attendance is not important; it is important and will be discussed in the next segment of this chapter. We shall discuss religion now, however, without reference to church attendance.

Religion plays an indispensable role in the life of the adolescent and is most effective when it stems from early childhood religious experiences. Religious feeling enables the teen-ager to communicate with God as he perceives Him. Belief in the omnipresence of the Creator within himself and everywhere in the universe gives the youngster security that he needs especially during crises, times of doubt, in periods of stress.

Adolescence is normally a period of searching for the "inner light," which represents personal insight into God. The teen-ager who searches for divine guidance but who learned little or nothing about God during the early years feels ordinarily a great void within himself that is difficult to fill, that can be filled only perhaps by profound religious conversion.

Religious faith, as contrasted with religious feeling, is

taken for granted by most youngsters during the middle years of childhood. Adolescence, however, brings on questions and doubts about religious faith. Teen-agers seem to realize suddenly that they do not understand much of what they previously accepted on faith. They wonder about the nature of God, the nature of man, the relationship of God to man and to the universe. They wonder, for example, whether God is a person, or a power, or a spirit—or whether He exists at all. They argue with one another about religious dogma, quarrel with their parents if the parents will listen to them. Wise parents do listen patiently and accept the teen-ager's religious confusion as being normal—which it is.

The argumentative teen-ager is actually trying to find his way through a spiritual thicket and uses his parents and friends as sounding boards. Some parents think, almost always erroneously, that the teen-ager is becoming an atheist or an agnostic at best and that their efforts to bring him up as a devoutly religious being have gone for naught. Consequently, they either refuse to hear his verbalized confusions or they deliver a scathing lecture, shame him into feeling guilty for entertaining religious doubts. These kinds of parental attitudes do not help the teen-ager; rather, they convince him that his parents do not genuinely understand him.

Studies show that teen-agers retain their religious beliefs, as a rule, in spite of adolescent doubts and confusions. Differences appear between the sexes in this respect. Girls, who mature earlier than boys and seem more stable emotionally, go to church more often and more consistently than boys and cling more tenaciously to religious faith. This pattern reflects perhaps the girls' passive, feminine role in the American culture, which expects girls to conform to social and religious pressures more than boys. Girls who seriously question their religious faith—most of them do question it during early adolescence—continue going through formal religious rites without rebelling. Boys, on the other hand, react more aggressively, refuse sometimes to go to church or to participate in other religious rites. This unwelcome behavior is usually short-lived, however, if the parents understand it, accept it, know it will pass.

Teen-agers vary greatly in their religious faith, be it Catholic, Protestant, Jewish, another religion, or no religion at all. Adolescents' stated religious faith ranges therefore from "none" to "extremely devout"; most youngsters are "middle-of-the-roaders," whom we may call "typical" or "average." A word picture of the typical American teen-ager's religious feeling, faith, and behavior was composed by Dr. H. H. Remmers, Director of the Purdue Opinion Panel, on the basis of thousands of high school students' responses:

"The typical American teen-ager today retains a favorable attitude toward the church, attends services about once a week and says prayers once or twice a day. His religious beliefs usually agree with those of his parents. If there is disagreement between the parents, the adolescent is more likely to agree with his mother's religious values than with those of his father. This makes him more of a churchgoer, since the typical mother of a teen-age child attends at least twice a month, while the father does not usually go to church that often.

"The average teen-ager thinks of God not as a person but as an omnipotent and omniscient bodiless spirit who exists everywhere. On the average, the teen-ager believes faith serves better than logic in solving life's important problems. He feels that his prayers are sometimes answered. He believes in the hereafter and expects his place there to be determined by his conduct here on earth. He believes that God guided or inspired the writing of the Bible, and that a good human society could not be built without such supernatural help."[3]

Recognize the ways in which church attendance and participation in church activities benefit teen-agers. Teenage boys and girls who as children attended church frequently and participated in religious activities continue

---

[3] From *The American Teenager* by H. H. Remmers and D. EL Radler, pp. 155-156, copyright © 1957 by H. H. Remmers, reprinted by special permission of the publishers, The Bobbs-Merrill Company, Inc.

doing so as a rule during adolescence. Church attendance is not necessarily correlated with moral conduct, according to youth studies; yet it can play a very important role in the life of the adolescent. First, exposure to religious teaching reinforces the teen-ager's sense of right and wrong. Second, belonging to a peer group that believes religion is important and church attendance is worthwhile helps him identify with boys and girls who respect the community's need for conventional religious behavior in youth. Third, youth activities at church and those sponsored by the church in the community provide wholesome, constructive outlets for the adolescent's energies and aggressive drives. They enable him to have a good time with his age-mates under competent, conscientious adult supervision. Fourth, youngsters find often in the ministry masculine figures with whom they can identify, thereby fortifying their own ego-strength. Such identification is most likely to occur in the boy whose father is absent from the home— by death, divorce, separation, or occupation—or is present but emotionally divorced from the family. Fifth, religious convictions, which are often reinforced by church attendance, reassure the teen-ager that it is not necessary to compromise his faith to please his peers. This knowledge is important. Studies of sexual promiscuity among teen-agers show, for example, that religious ideals and loyalty to parents are the two reasons girls state most often as the reason for avoiding premarital intercourse, far outdistancing fear of pregnancy and fear of venereal infection as motives for remaining virginal.

I think the benefits that adolescents derive from going to church and participating in church youth activities are sufficient reasons in themselves for parents to encourage their teen-agers in this direction.

As parents, be good examples of moral and spiritual strength. Teen-agers need parents whom they love and admire even though they are moving gradually away from them and into the wider community. They need parents who are morally clean and spiritually strong. They need parents who love and respect each other and who genuinely cherish their children. They need parents who are really interested in their youngsters as persons, as individuals, as adolescents. They need parents who set good examples for them by contributing of themselves and their worldly goods to mankind and to God. They need parents who are, by virtue of their actual beliefs and daily conduct, genuinely worthy of being loved, respected, revered.

Conscientious parents hope and pray that they genuinely deserve their children's love and respect. This parental attitude is probably more important than any other in helping a teen-ager grow up.

Review of major points

1. Understand the developmental changes that occur normally during adolescence.
2. Appreciate the adolescent's need to discover his moral and spiritual self.
3. Recognize the peer group's power to influence behavior and its inability to change values.
4. Understand the traditional values of the adolescent society.
5. Understand the inconsistencies among the teen-ager's moral knowledge, actual moral beliefs, stated beliefs, and conduct.
6. Appreciate the value of religion in the life of the teen-ager.
7. Recognize the ways in which church attendance and participation in church activities help teen-agers grow up.
8. As parents, be good examples of moral and spiritual strength.

SUMMARY

This chapter discussed moral and spiritual values in the lives of adolescents and suggested ways parents can help the teen-ager reinforce his moral and spiritual values.

The next chapter will deal with citizenship during adolescence and suggest ways parents can help their teenager become an effective citizen.

Chapter 14

The Responsibilities of Citizenship

CITIZENSHIP IN THE United States of America implies human rights more precious and privileges more extensive than citizenship in any other nation; at the same time, however, it requires more thought and consideration of the civic and moral responsibilities of the individual.

American citizenship in its broadest sense means many things. It means voting, enjoying liberty and freedom, paying taxes. It means taking pride and active interest in the neighborhood, the schools, the community. It means striving to understand one's obligations to society, learning the deeper meaning of freedom through responsible daily living, mastering the instruments of self-government through self-control and self-discipline. It means understanding, respecting, obeying the law, supporting the law-making bodies and the law enforcement agencies. It means assuming responsibility for one's convictions and conduct, contributing ideas and services for the good of the community, being informed and sensitive to local, state, national, and world affairs that affect America. It means being patriotic and loyal to the United States, serving in the armed forces if needed. It means contributing in every feasible way to the peace and welfare of humanity throughout the world.

Citizenship in the United States is closely related to morality and spirituality in the individual; indeed, effective citizenship is valued highly, being almost synonymous with moral responsibility. The preceding chapter, which discussed ways of reinforcing sound moral and spiritual values during adolescence, may therefore be considered an integral part of this discussion rather than a preliminary to it.

America's parents want generally to see their youngsters grow up to be effective citizens who contribute to the welfare of the great democratic community that is

America. The suggestions that follow are intended to help them fulfill that desire.

Recognize the need for education and training for the responsibilities of citizenship. Good citizenship involves doing what is right and not doing what is wrong. This concept may seem simple, but it is actually very complex. How does one know what is right and what is wrong? It is often very difficult in our culture to answer this question because of the nature of democratic living: what is "right" in one situation may be "wrong" in another one. An act is rarely absolutely right or absolutely wrong when one understands all the facts surrounding the act Therefore, the rules for good citizenship in a democracy are not as simple as those handed down by dictators in totalitarian nations.

Democracy is basically an *accepting* political and social philosophy. Respect for oneself and others is an essential attitude for living successfully in America. This democratic society encourages a wide variety of political, religious, and social beliefs and behaviors that would not be permitted in a totalitarian regime: freedom of religion, freedom of speech, freedom of the press, freedom to criticize and petition the government, freedom of movement, the right to public trial by jury, the right to bear arms peaceably, and many others. Rights and privileges such as these are contingent upon effective self-government by the people, a condition that necessarily implies duties and responsibilities of America's citizens.

Wholesome, positive attitudes toward citizenship responsibilities do not come naturally; they must be learned. If they are to be learned effectively, they must be thoroughly taught. This task is a large and important one that involves parents, the school, and the community.

Appreciate the roles of the home, the school, and the community in preparing teen-agers for effective citizen' ship. Parents play the starring role in educating and training the child for citizenship. They mold his mind and emotions, shape his attitudes, plant the seeds of belief and faith in his life during the formative years and cultivate them throughout childhood. They may play this role effectively or ineffectively, for good or for evil, to make a good citizen or a bad one. Most parents play this role well; some of them, unfortunately, play it poorly, and others abandon the role entirely, leaving the youngster to shift for himself.

The child learns additional fundamentals of citizenship ordinarily from neighborhood adults, playmates, and friends, who may be considered extensions of his own household. If parents work effectively with the child, these other persons play a distinctly secondary role, supplementing and complementing the parents' teachings. If the parents ignore or neglect the child, however, these outsiders may be the youngster's main sources of education and training for citizenship.

The school plays a very important role in citizenship education and training. Teachers and other professional school personnel spend a great deal of time and energy imparting information, attitudes, concepts, and values re-garding the rights, privileges, duties, and responsibilities of citizens at school and in the wider community. These teachings are translated into everyday living situations and determine the basic principles that govern the educational process in the classroom, in the student government, and throughout the life of the student body on campus. Thus, the well-regulated public school in America becomes a laboratory for democratic living, a practical training ground for effective citizenship.[1]

But the school is often relatively ineffective at educating and training for citizenship when compared with the home. Teen-agers whose parents teach them continually to be good citizens at home are usually good citizens at school. The power of parents to educate is even more apparent, however, in youngsters whose conditioning at home is negative, destructive, antisocial. These individuals are

---

[1] Several important examples of education and training for effective citizenship in America's high schools were discussed earlier. See pp. 138-143.

usually limited in academic ability and put forth little or no effort in school. They regard teachers generally with contempt or an air of tolerance at best. They are often truant and uncooperative, occasionally impudent and unmanageable. The parental influence is readily apparent in their behavior at school and in some cases is demonstrated dramatically in the community. The following news item (with names of persons and places changed to respect right of privacy) illustrates this point:

Father, Son Arrested in Burglary Ring

A father and his 16-year-old son were arrested yesterday in the investigation of an extensive auto theft and burglary ring in the St. Francis area. Three other persons were taken into custody.

Jack Johnson, 44, and his son, Peter, were questioned by police in the investigation of 70 garage burglaries in the past four months. Police said about $15,000 worth of loot was recovered from Johnson's home and that of Walter Hanks, 42, his neighbor and alleged accomplice.

Johnson and his teen-age son were implicated after police arrested two juveniles in a stolen car who led them to the Johnson home.

Recovered loot include radios, cameras, appliances, tape recorders, and other items police said were taken from cars and garages.

Johnson and Hanks were booked on suspicion of receiving stolen property. Peter was booked on suspicion of grand theft auto.

This case of a parent's unwholesome influence on his son is more extreme than most; yet it is milder than some. It illustrates the point that parents can teach their offspring to be bad citizens as well as good ones. Few parents do this as blatantly as Mr. Johnson. Yet many parents unwittingly teach their youngsters negative citizenship attitudes by leveling irrational, unwarranted verbal criticism at the government, the public schools, constructive community agencies; by condemning national leaders who think differently from themselves; by decrying continually the "crookedness" of public officials; by complaining incessantly about high taxes, the high cost of living, the "big guys on Wall Street who have all the money" or "the labor unions that are ruining the nation's economy"; by cheating the government on income tax returns; by failing to go to the polls and vote; and in many other ways. In other words, there are many ways to teach poor citizenship attitudes besides training a youngster for a life of crime.

One might imagine that teen-agers who are negatively oriented at home toward the responsibilities of citizenship would change their values when exposed to the positive approach that is generally taught and practiced at school. In reality, they behave generally according to school rules and regulations, but they rarely change their values. Values that were implanted in early childhood and strengthened during the middle years remain (as was explained in the previous chapter) usually throughout adolescence even though superficial changes in behavior are made to conform with peer group expectancies. It makes little difference to the negatively oriented teen-ager that his citizenship values are destructive rather than constructive, undesirable rather than wholesome. Once planted and well-rooted, they grow and thrive. This is the reason why the home is more important than the school in educating and teaming young Americans to become good citizens—or bad ones. This is the reason why parents must understand the fact that they themselves are the primary sources of good citizenship attitudes— and unwholesome ones—in their children.

Teach self-control and self-discipline through demo-erotic family living. "Democracy begins in the home," says Dr. Paul Popenoe, retired Director of the American Institute of Family Relations. "This fact now, more than ever, needs to be recognized by every parent. If the home fails in its job, the schools have no machinery which can possibly be expected to undo the harm already done. In a well-organized family the child learns by example and by daily practice that there is a balance between privileges and responsibilities in life."

Studies show convincingly that youngsters who grow up in a democratic home are generally more successful in school and in society than are those from either an autocratic home or one which has no effective rules or regulations—the *laissez-faire* home. They adjust better to school and community demands, display more self-control, better self-discipline. They get in trouble less frequently, contribute more time and effort to school and community service, take more interest in the world about them. They show more initiative, greater creativity, better potential for leadership in a free society. These are the kinds of qualities America needs in her citizens.

Characteristics of teen-agers from democratic homes contrast sharply with those found often in adolescents from the autocratic home, where the parents "lay down the law" for the children, enforce it with threats and grim determination, mete out harsh punishment whenever they discover an infraction of the rules. This parental philosophy says in effect to the teen-ager, "Do as you're told. That is the only way you can stay out of trouble." It places all the emphasis on conforming to the parents' dictates, none on thinking creatively. This kind of family living teaches not democracy but authoritarianism or, even worse, totalitarianism.

Different still are the results commonly observed in teen-agers from *laissez-faire* homes, which have no rules or regulations that anyone takes seriously, not even the parents. These boys and girls are usually confused about ethics, beliefs, values at home and in the wider community. They lack adequate social judgment, which is not surprising since this quality originates ordinarily in carefully regulated family interaction. They show little awareness of or appreciation for society's laws, because they have not experienced rules at home.

A household without rules and regulations is like a football team that tries to play without rules, without yard markers, without boundaries, without end zones: no one knows who is supposed to go where or do what, if any-thing. Obviously, there must be rules, boundaries, players, referees, rewards for gains, penalties for infractions, and all the other necessities if a football game is to be played sensibly. The same principle applies to the game of family living.

The problem America's parents face in this matter is to make democracy work in the home, applying the principles of democratic living to the family unit. This means regarding each family member as a full-fledged player on the team, a human being who deserves respect and consideration equal to that given everyone else and who contributes his share to the total team effort. It means encouraging each family member to consider thoughtfully the problems that the household faces, to contribute ideas, to discuss his and others' ideas in the family group, and to try to come up with reasonable, workable solutions to the problems. It means discussing also the need for rules and regulations by which all members of the family must abide, listening to the proposals of each member, coming to tentative conclusions and, finally, establishing reasonable rules and regulations. It means enforcing these self-imposed laws, preferably by family-determined methods. Parents must, of course, guide such procedures and remain the final authority in all matters that require such authority.

Most of the parent-adolescent problems discussed thus far in this book should be carefully considered by parents and teen-agers together in a democratic manner. Here are some examples: How late should a teen-ager stay out on a date? When should a boy and a girl start going steady? What should be the teen-ager's responsibilities if he uses the family car for a date? Who should pay for insurance and operating costs on a teen-ager's car? Should a teen-ager be expected to work and save money to help pay his way through college? Should a teen-ager who has a part-time job be expected to buy his own clothes? What "strings," if any, should be attached to a weekly allow-ance? These are but a few questions you might discuss with your teen-ager. You may want to formulate different problems or ask your youngster to state those that concern him now. In any case, friendly discussion of teenagers' problems prevents misunderstandings and leads often to increased cooperation by the teen-ager at home, at school, and in the community.

Teach youngsters to respect the law, to obey it, and to support law enforcement. Teen-agers who respect thenown parents—the primary authority figures in their lives —respect generally all persons in positions of authority. This attitude is especially common among adolescents who live in a democratic home where the family members formulate the rules and determine penalties for infractions of the rules. Parents are in command, of course, but they are not autocrats or dictators. Nor are they disinterested owners of the home who want their youngsters to leave them alone and run their own lives without parental guidance.

Laws of a democratic nation are the creations of its citizenry, just as rules in the democratic family are products of its members. America's laws are made usually after careful study and consideration by many interested persons, some of whom represent large segments of the population. Laws exist in a democracy to protect the people and to promote the common welfare. They are laws of the people, by the people, for the people. They deserve everyone's respect.

Many laws exist that are in conflict with the desires, wishes, ambitions of some people and are, therefore, being continually broken. In fact, some adults show little respect at all for laws; for them, getting caught is the only disgrace for breaking laws. Their excuses for lawbreaking vary but include usually the suggestion that the law they broke was a bad one which should not have existed in the first place. They are right in some instances; nevertheless, this attitude demonstrates disrespect for duly constituted law. The proper way to deal with an undesirable law is to proceed through legal channels and have it revised or eliminated. In the meantime, citizens should try to abide by it.

Law enforcement authorities are needed in a democratic society to enforce the laws of the people, who pay taxes to pay for law enforcement. It is strange that law enforcement authorities are often opposed or subverted by many well-meaning but misguided citizens who unwittingly support the lawbreaker, not the law enforcer. One reason for this apparent inconsistency is perhaps that many people see unconsciously in the contest between lawbreaker and law enforcer a reenactment of the traditional contest between the child who misbehaves and the parent who detects the misbehavior and punishes the child. They identify themselves with the lawbreaker, sympathize with him, hope he will outwit the law enforcer. This pattern represents an immaturity, of course, in the adult's thinking, suggests unresolved childhood relationships with his own parents regarding misbehavior, detection, and punishment.

Parents are wise who uphold law enforcement authorities and support their efforts generously. This parental attitude produces greater respect for law and for law enforcement in the teen-ager's mind. This is not to say, of course, that law enforcement officers and agencies are perfect; naturally, they make mistakes as every one else does. Parents, too, make mistakes. So do teen-agers.

Parents should themselves set good examples in citizenship for their teen-agers. The attitudes parents demonstrate become the teen-ager's attitudes; the values parents cherish become the teen-ager's values. The effective parent is law-abiding. He rarely if ever practices what he abhors in his preachments. He does not tell his teen-ager in effect, "Do as I say, not as I do." He knows that law-abiding adolescents come ordinarily from homes with law-abiding parents. He knows that the easiest and most effective way to make his youngster a good citizen is to be one himself.

Teach teen-agers to assume responsibility for their conduct. Adolescents in modern, civilized cultures are necessarily discouraged from assuming the responsibilities of adulthood; that is, they are encouraged to postpone adult patterns such as marriage, for example, until they have completed their education, secured a job that pays a living wage and offers good prospects for future advancement, and demonstrated in other ways that they are mature enough to meet the responsibilities of adulthood. Parents must adopt this attitude generally toward their teen-agers because it is realistic and practical. Yet it is also unrealistic and impractical from the teen-ager's point of view. He sees himself as being sexually mature; biologically capable of marriage and parenthood; physically able to work and earn a living; as mature emotionally as most adults, more mature perhaps than many of them; more "open-minded," more optimistic, more flexible than most adults. He thinks sometimes that adults envy teen-agers, do not want them to have fun, want them to behave as if they were still children.

Adults, on the other hand, feel sometimes that teen-agers want to be treated as adults but want to behave as irresponsible children. Dr. Virginia Armon, chief psychologist for the Pasadena (California) Child Guidance Clinic, explains this dilemma as centering around the teenager's need to break away from home while he still yearns for the protection of the home. "The adolescent," she explains, "needs adult freedom to do the things he wants to do, but at the same time he wants to avoid disagreeable adult responsibilities. This contradiction often infuriates parents. Yet the contradiction is natural in an age of transition, which is what adolescence is. Meanwhile the teen-ager is trying, without much success, to live up to four different sets of standards at once: the standards of his parents; the standards of his fellow teen-agers; the standards of the adult world away from home; and his own newly forming individual inner standards." Dr. Armon illustrates her thesis with the example of a teen-ager who wants the adult freedom to smoke but who avoids the responsibility of earning the money to pay for his cigarettes.

Parents delay unnecessarily adolescents' assumption of responsibility for their conduct in many cases by denying the youngsters the privilege of making their own decisions and acting on them. Some parents say to teen-agers: "You are too young to know what's best for you." "You do the dreaming; I'll do the deciding." "You're not old enough to decide such an important matter." "You're still wet behind the ears." "You're getting too big for your britches." Such comments as these show unjustifiable disrespect for teen-agers, who deserve parental understanding and consideration. They represent attempts by the parent to belittle the youngster, to shame him into remaining child-like rather than asserting himself. Sometimes these kinds of remarks backfire on the parent when the teen-ager goes out of his way to prove that the parent's opinion of him is wrong. Consider Linda, for example, a seventeen-year-old girl whose mother forbade her to have dates because, in Mother's words, "You're not old enough to know anything about boys." Linda had secret dates and got pregnant out of wedlock. Mother was shocked, as one might expect, but Linda was delighted to be an expectant mother because she had proved Mother wrong and had convinced herself that she was really a full-fledged female!

Parents may encourage teen-agers to accept responsibility for their conduct by discussing with them their problems before they decide what to do about them. Teenagers need to talk over their concerns with their parents and, on the basis of honest, frank discussions, decide what to do and what to avoid. Teen-agers should, with competent parental advice and counsel, make their own decisions and act on them, knowing they must accept the consequences. If a decision proves to have been wrong, the teen-ager should be helped by the parent to profit from his error in judgment. If a decision proves to have been wise, the teen-ager gains additional self-confidence and moves another step forward toward maturity. In either case, the teen-ager accepts responsibility for his conduct that was carefully considered beforehand rather than assigning blame or credit—as the case may be—to the parent or to someone else other than himself.

Encourage your teen-ager to contribute ideas and services for community improvement. The capable, creative youngster has much to offer the community generally in ideas and services. I think parents should encourage adolescents to do everything they can to make the community a better place in which to live; indeed, this may be rightfully regarded a responsibility of parents.

Teen-agers can often render outstanding service which the community genuinely needs; furthermore, they may demonstrate considerable initiative and originality in discovering new ways to fill community needs. Here, for example, are some services teen-agers in various communities across the nation are performing:

Community clean-up. High school students contribute their services four successive Saturday mornings in the spring to pick up tin cans, paper sacks, and other litter strewn about the community and its environs by "litter-bugs." At the end of the clean-up campaign, the participants celebrate their achievement with a dance at the high school, sponsored by a local adult service organization.

Babysitting service. Teen-age members of a girls' organization contribute their services as baby-sitters for infants and children who are physically or mentally handicapped. All cash rewards that they receive become contributions to the community hospital for research into prevention of handicaps.

Public health information service. Members of a teen-age boys' club walk voluntarily from house to house distributing invitations from an adult service organization to all persons in the community to get a free chest X-ray.

Youth legislative information service. A teen-age group studies proposed state and national legislation that pertains to children and youth, analyzes it, and disseminate analyses to other youth groups, urging them to make their feelings known to the legislators.

Service to the church. Young people serve the church in many ways. One group of teen-agers contributed many evenings and Saturdays to help clean and remodel the interior of the church and paint the exterior. Another group helped build a new church, acting as helpers for carpenters, bricklayers, plasterers and other skilled craftsmen, who donated their services too.

Future teachers' services. A group of teen-agers who expect to become teachers offer their services free to younger pupils who need tutoring help with school work.

Book drive. A boys' club initiates and carries out an annual community book drive that last year netted more than 4,000 usable books for children to be donated to a children's hospital.

These are but a few of the hundreds of activities in which teen-agers participate to contribute their ideas and services for the betterment of the community. Parents are wise who encourage their adolescent sons and daughters to participate in such activities because participation serves the common good and constitutes good training for effective citizenship.[2]

Encourage your teen-ager to be curious and informed about local, state, national, and world affairs that may affect him as a citizen of the United States. Modern methods of mass communication—television, radio, newspapers, etc.—make it easy for people to be informed about what is going on in the world. Studies show, however, that in spite of the continual flow of information through mass communication media, most people have only a hazy understanding of state, national, and international affairs. This is unfortunate, especially in a democratic nation such as ours, where each individual has the right to voice his opinion and every qualified adult has the privilege of making his opinion felt through the polls. America must better educate future voters if democratic processes are to be successful.

Model legislatures in high schools and youth organizations provide some training in responsible lawmaking at the state level. In some states, for example, the legislature turns over its facilities to a teen-agers' model legislature sponsored by a youth service organization such as the

[2] *Parents Magazine* has for several years given recognition and awards annually to local youth groups throughout the nation who serve the community in interesting and useful ways. For information, write Youth Group Achievement Awards, *Parents Magazine,* 52 Vanderbilt Avenue, New York 17, New York.

YMCA. The youngsters who participate have been elected to the mock legislature through democratic procedures and represent constituencies as do adult legislators. They propose legislation, debate the issues, vote according to their convictions. Records show that many laws passed by teen-agers in mock sessions of the California legislature have later been introduced and passed by the regular legislature, indicating that the youngsters have rather mature judgment regarding certain needed legislation.

Teen-age reading tastes as revealed in a study by the American Library Association suggest changing interests of today's adolescents. They have shifted definitely in recent years from fiction to the nonfiction, with emphasis on world political and sociological problems. This interest in world problems and concern with ways of solving them is heightened probably by television, which makes it possible for youngsters to see documentary evidence of the problems as well as hear about them. Incidentally, the shift in reading habits of teen-agers parallels that of adults.

Teen-agers have been accused of being generally un-aware of important world issues about which citizens in a democracy should be informed. There is undoubtedly some justification for this attitude when one considers the entire adolescent population. Studies reveal, however, that intelligent adolescents are usually aware, informed, and thoughtful—more so perhaps than most adults. Here, for example, are some excerpts from teen-agers' replies to the question, *"What do you think will be the most important development in the world in your lifetime?"*

HELEN: I think the most important development in my lifetime will be a workable disarmament plan that will permit the people of the world to live in peace with one another.

DAVID: I think if we can achieve lasting peace, this will be the most important development. World population and food problems probably will remain problems throughout my lifetime.

BILL: The explorations of space by man will be most important. However, I hope too to see the entire world become free from tyranny.

STEVE: World peace. If we don't establish lasting world peace in the next fifty years, there will be no humanity left to worry about.

DICK: Man in space. However, I would prefer to see world peace if it is possible.

LORRAINE: I'm afraid the race for space will mean using another planet for military purposes. Frankly, the most important development in the world for me will be a continued hope in the humanity of man, a hope that perhaps somewhere a doctor will discover a means of bringing out the goodness in man.

Teen-agers who view human affairs throughout the world thoughtfully, seriously, with continuing curiosity and interest will probably become the most useful citizens of tomorrow's America. Parents should do whatever they can to encourage them in this respect.

Teach your teen-ager to be patriotic and loyal to the United States. Patriotism and loyalty to one's country are important values that should be learned during the formative years of life, reinforced during middle childhood, internalized, analyzed, and defined during adolescence. Parents who really want their children to become good citizens will usually promote this process as a matter of course.

Patriotism and loyalty do not mean merely reciting the oath of allegiance, saluting the flag, or singing the national anthem, which are admittedly important acts but do not necessarily connote true patriotism. "Genuine patriotism calls for a proper balance between factual understanding and emotional conviction," says Dr. C. C. Trillingham, former president of the American Association of School Administrators and head of Los Angeles County's public schools. "Patriotism is most effective when it is positive and thus emphasizes what we believe in and what we are for."

Some well-intentioned but perhaps misguided citizens think patriotism means hating ideas that conflict with their own and condemning people who entertain those ideas. They describe their opposition as being "suspicious," "traitorous," "subversive," "un-American," or some other disreputable term without adequate evidence that these labels really fit. They describe top governmental leaders—the President of the United States, the Justices of the Supreme Court, the Secretary of State, and many others —as "willing conspirators who work hand-in-glove with this nation's enemies." These individuals, sometimes termed "superpatriots," feel definitely that they are effectively fighting the enemy by displaying this brand of patriotism.

"Too often patriotism is displayed as a tirade of things we are against," Dr. Trillingham declares. "The physical manifestations of patriotism, such as the pledge of allegiance, will probably not mean too much to the participants unless they are based upon deep understanding which grows out of inner meanings."

Dr. Trillingham believes patriotic ritual has definite value; he insists, however, that patriotic behavior in the individual extends far beyond ritual. The truly patriotic American, he declares, behaves day by day in these ways:

"He is law-abiding, respects regulations as having come from the people and as being for the good of the people. If he believes a law is not a good law, he works through orderly processes for its revision or abolition.

"He has an informed opinion and expresses it through discussion in his own community and through his vote at the polls.

"He gives service as his abilities and energies may be needed on school and community problems, by being a committee member, by running for office, by contributing money or materials as the situation may require, by performing military service when this becomes necessary.

"His faith in American ideals leads him to work in harmony with others toward maintaining the principles upon which our nation is based: the worth and dignity of the individual; the enjoyment of basic freedom by everyone; concern for the general welfare; and the improvability of human existence through cooperative effort and good will."

Dr. Trillingham's definition of the patriot in terms of his everyday behavior is one parents will be wise to observe as they urge teen-agers to be patriotic, loyal American citizens.

Help your son prepare for military service. Every able-bodied American male teen-ager is probably destined for a period of military service, according to the chief counsel of the Selective Service. World affairs make compulsory military training and service necessary. Parents should recognize the inevitability of military service for their able-bodied teen-age son and take a positive attitude toward the experience rather than dreading or deploring it. Naturally, there are risks involved; yet statistics reveal that the risks are no greater in peacetime military service than in college attendance or in normal everyday living. Parents should encourage their teen-ager to look forward to military service as an important learning experience, not as time lost from living.

Parents of teen-agers who expect to go to college may be understandably concerned about the effect selective service will have on educational plans. The American Personnel and Guidance Association advises, "If a student makes good grades in his freshman year in college and has a score of 70 or more on the Selective Service College Qualification Test, he will probably be deferred until graduation."

Parents should ask the draft board or the college to furnish details on the Selective Service College Qualification Test, which is administered twice each year, usually in November and April. Parents are warned, however, that a youngster is permitted to take this test only once; his first and only score is therefore the deciding factor.

Regardless of his academic status, the teen-ager must register with his local draft board within five days after his eighteenth birthday. Within a few days he will receive his individual Registration Certificate, which will include his Selective Service number. Later, he will receive a lengthy document, the Classification Questionnaire, which he must complete and return to the draft board within ten days. The board will then determine his draft status and notify him of his classification.

High school seniors wonder sometimes whether they should complete military service first and then go to college. There is no single answer to this question. Military service is a maturing experience for many youths, makes them more serious about their studies when they go to college. Some individuals however, find it difficult to return to school when they have been away from it for a while. This problem is one the teen-ager should talk through with his parents, his high school counselor, and perhaps with the admissions counselor at the college.

The APGA offers this suggestion to parents of the teen-ager who wants to go to college first: "He may be able to assure his deferment until graduation by joining the ROTC program. Some colleges have a unit in the Army, Navy, or Air Force Reserve Training Corps, and there are other training programs in addition to ROTC available to college students." Parents are advised to consult the catalog of the college their son will attend to find out whether or not it has an ROTC unit or other suitable program.

Help your teen-ager prepare for intelligent exercise of the voting privilege. American citizens must be at least twenty-one years old before they can vote in national elections and, with some exceptions, must also be that old before they can vote in state elections. Legislators believe generally that a large majority of young people are not yet ready to vote before their twenty-first birthday because they lack adequate maturity. The more capable teen-agers do not often agree with this point of view. Here is a statement by a very bright fourteen-year-old high school girl in behalf of the franchise for eighteen-year olds:

Why can't eighteen-year-olds vote? They could do much for our country with their intelligence, integrity, enthusiasm and high ideals.

Right now, our country is worried about the direction the cold war is taking. If we start our people voting early enough we can ensure their loyalty to our government. We know that this loyalty is necessary to keep the cold war from turning into a hot war. Yet we won't let the eighteen-year-olds vote.

We also know that the broader the base of the electorate, the more representative and democratic our government will be. When eighteen-year-olds can't vote, our electorate is smaller, and therefore our government is less democratic!

Our government was founded partly on the statement "No taxation without representation." Yet many of our eighteen-year-olds are taxed but can't vote. And eighteen-year-olds also have many of the other duties of an adult citizen. They may work, drive cars and marry, among other things. If drafted, they may shed their very lifeblood for their country. Yet they can't vote!

A few of our states have faced these facts fairly. Now, in Kentucky and Georgia, one may vote at eighteen; Alaska, nineteen; and Hawaii twenty. I think all states (and the United States) should lower the voting age so eighteen-year-olds can vote.

This young teen-ager's argument has some merit, especially as it applies to the more mature, intellectually capable, morally responsible adolescent, who is often better qualified to vote than many adults. The following statement from a mature woman illustrates this point:

My nephew is twenty years old. Soon he will graduate from college, and the same day he will receive his commission as an officer in the Marine Air Corps. The following day he will be married.

Now, under our outmoded laws, he is still classified as a minor child: he cannot even obtain his marriage license without his mother going along to sign her permission for him to marry!

He has his rating already as a commercial pilot; the government will probably trust <u>him</u> with million-dollar airplanes long before he reaches the age that is out of the "minor child" classification.

I cite this case to show you how outmoded the "adulthood at twenty-one" concept is now. Our young men should be treated as *men;* they should not be insulted by the stigma of being children until they have attained their twenty-first birthday. They should be granted the rights and privileges of adulthood at eighteen.

I would favor lowering the legal age for adulthood to eighteen years if I believed even half of the nation's eighteen-year-olds are capable individually of exercising sound judgment in times of crisis, which is when the weight of votes counts the most. In my opinion, most eighteen-year-olds are still influenced too much by the peer group to think independently about political, economic, sociologic matters. There are some youngsters who would obviously be capable, competent voters even before they reach their eighteenth birthday; they are, however, the exceptions, the unusual ones. I think it would be unwise to lower the voting age for everyone— including mentally retarded minors—to accommodate the more capable individuals.

Parents can help their teen-ager appreciate the franchise by themselves making maximum use of their voting privilege, by registering periodically, by going regularly to the polls. The example they set by exercising their right to vote serves as a pattern for the teen-ager's behavior in the future when he, too, will be old enough legally to vote.

Encourage your teen-ager to respect and protect himself so he can fulfill his responsibilities as a citizen. The automobile kills more American teen-agers than any disease or any other instrument of death and maims many thousands each year. This disturbing fact was discussed in an earlier chapter; it is repeated here to illustrate a point: youngsters must take care of themselves if they are to stay alive and enjoy reasonably good health—two conditions that seem prerequisite to meeting the duties and responsibilities of citizenship. The dead teen-ager cannot become an effective citizen. The maimed teen-ager may or may not be able to fulfill the responsibilities of citizenship, depending on the nature and extent of his injuries. Ronald, a seventeen-year-old senior in a nearby high school was killed instantly last spring when he lost control of his car on the freeway and crashed it against a concrete abutment. Gary, his eighteen-year-old passenger and companion, was injured critically, suffering severe brain damage that rendered him permanently mentally deficient and partially paralyzed the rest of his life. Ronald's death was tragic, of course; yet Gary's injury is perhaps more pitiful, for he was the president of the high school student body, an honor student, a potential leader in the community. Now he will spend the rest of his life in a state-supported institution for the mentally deficient, where he will require special care of the type that is ordinarily reserved for infants and small children.

This story of Ronald and Gary is neither pleasant nor very unusual. Communities across the nation have their Ronalds and their Garys each year; the killing and maiming of teen-agers in automobiles goes on continually as if it were necessary, inevitable, routine.

The tragic loss of teen-age potential for effective citizenship is serious and widespread not only by virtue of the motor vehicles massacre but also by other disablers and destroyers, such as marijuana, narcotics, and crime.

Studies show that many teen-agers "try out" marijuana cigarettes as a result of adolescent curiosity: they want simply to find out how it feels. Most youngsters try them once, satisfy their curiosity, never return to them. These are the well-balanced, emotionally secure individuals. Some youngsters, on the other hand, get a false feeling of self-assurance and grandeur from marijuana and are soon dependent on it.

The young marijuana user searches eventually for a more powerful agent and becomes a prospective customer, therefore, of the narcotics pusher. He would be wise to resist temptation, use only marijuana or tobacco. However, he may give in to the pusher's urging and start using heroin. If he does, he is "hooked," probably for life. His body becomes habituated quickly to the drug and needs it to function. If the unfortunate youngster cannot get heroin, he suffers seemingly endless hours of suffocating nausea, agonizing pain. These are the symptoms of withdrawal—the nightmare of "kicking the habit."

Narcotics addiction leads frequently to crime because "feeding the habit" is expensive, and the user is usually not able to make an honest living. He must rob, steal, burglarize, cheat, patronize, solicit, prostitute himself, kill —anything to support his habit. Law enforcement agencies estimate conservatively that more than half of all crimes and criminal offenses in urban America today involve narcotics addicts.

Youngsters who continue smoking marijuana (which is habit-forming but not physiologically addicting) and those who become addicted to narcotics are usually found to have been emotionally unstable as children, rejected and neglected at home, unsuccessful, unhappy, and unwanted at school and in the community. Studies show that in eight out of ten cases, the basic causes of such delinquent behavior can be traced generally to the home and specifically to parental inadequacies. These youngsters will probably never be good citizens. Their parents are not proud of them, will never be. Nor should the parents be proud of themselves: they failed to give their children a good start in life; they failed to help them grow up.

If you really want to help your teen-ager grow up, you will give him the facts about the dangers of using cigarettes (which almost invariably precede marijuana), liquor (which is involved in a large percentage of automobile crashes), and of experimenting with marijuana, narcotics, prostitution, sexual perversion, and the other shady, shabby sides of life. You will warn him of these dangers, suggest ways he may avoid them, keep him from hurting himself and others. These things you must do to fulfill your obligation as a parent and to insure his future as a responsible American citizen.

Review of major points

1. Recognize the need for education and training for the responsibilities of citizenship.
2. Appreciate the roles of the home, the school, and the community in preparing youngsters for effective citizenship.
3. Teach self-control and self-discipline through democratic family living.
4. Teach youngsters to respect the law, to obey it, and to support law enforcement.
5. Teach teen-agers to assume responsibility for their conduct.
6. Encourage your teen-ager to contribute ideas and services for community improvement.
7. Encourage your youngster to be interested in and informed about local, state, national, and world affairs that may affect him as a citizen of the United States.
8. Teach your teen-ager to be patriotic and loyal to the United States.
9. Help your son prepare for military service.
10. Help your youngster prepare for intelligent exercise of the voting privilege.
11. Encourage your youngster to respect and protect himself so he can fulfill his responsibilities as a citizen.

SUMMARY

This chapter discussed the responsibilities of citizenship in the United States of America and suggested ways parents can help their teen-ager learn to accept and fulfill these responsibilities.

The next chapter will deal with marriage and parenthood and will suggest ways parents can help their youngster prepare for the responsibilities of successful marriage and effective parenthood.

Chapter 15

Preparing for Marriage and Parenthood

MORE YOUNG PEOPLE marry at an early age today than ever before in our nation's history. Half of all marriages in modern America involve brides who are not yet twenty years old; some of them are not yet fifteen. The groom in half of all first marriages is not yet twenty-three years old.

Older teen-agers may marry without parental consent in many states. Twelve-year-old girls and fourteen-year-old boys may marry with parental consent in some states, but they rarely do.

Leaders of youth—educators, ministers, counselors—generally oppose teen-age marriages. They say most teen-agers lack qualities that successful marriage requires: maturity, adequate education, useful vocation, satisfactory income.

Parents today are asking: "What may we do to help our teen-agers grow up? How may we guide them to success and happiness in marriage?" The suggestions that follow may help answer these questions.

Understand the facts about marital failure and divorce in modern America. The divorce rate in the United States is the highest in the world; no other nation's rate comes close to it. Thousands of sermons have decried this fact, hundreds of articles have deplored it, and scores of books have reported investigations into it. They all seem to come to one common conclusion: our divorce rate is a national disgrace.

Being the most divorce-ridden country in the world is a dubious distinction; however, when one takes into account certain little-known facts that provide some reasons for the high divorce rate, he may find the situation less chaotic than it appears on the surface.

Dr. Lawrence Kubie, Clinical Professor of Psychiatry at Yale University's School of Medicine, dispels the

221

popular notion that America's high divorce rate results from twentieth-century laxity in morals. He demonstrates with carefully charted data that the divorce rate has risen in America during the twentieth century mainly because people are living longer than before.[1]

Many marriages that are now terminated by divorce would have been terminated by death some years ago. Before 1900, death was quite common between the ages of twenty and fifty years. Today, as a result of medical knowledge, the life expectancy for the American male is sixty-seven years; for the American female, it is seventy-three years. Heart disease and cancer, Dr. Kubie points out, have become the two main causes of death in the twentieth century for the same reason divorces have increased: people are living longer. People have more opportunity today to develop heart disease and get cancer.

Contrary to popular belief, the divorce rate in America has for several years been going down, not up. The United States Bureau of the Census reports that in 1940 there was one divorce in three marriages; in 1960, there was one divorce in four marriages. This drop of 8 per cent represents a very significant change in the divorce rate.

The average marriage today lasts longer than before and seems more successful. 1960's newlyweds, a Census Bureau spokesman declared recently, can expect to live through forty-three years of marriage; by contrast, 1900's newlyweds could expect to live only thirty-one years beyond the wedding ceremony. Thus, modern American marriages are faring better than uninformed alarmists would have one believe. This fact is surprising when one considers that today, thanks to increased mobility, many people are meeting and marrying who probably would have remained single—not by choice but by lack of opportunity to marry—a few generations ago. Furthermore, some persons with serious personality disorders who should not marry at all do get married today because they think social pressures demand it.

[1] See "Psychoanalysis and Marriage," by Lawrence S. Kubie, M.D., in *Neurotic Interaction in Marriage,* edited by Victor W. Eisenstein, M.D. (Basic Books: N.Y., 1956), pp. 10-15.

Perhaps the most significant development on the modern American marriage scene is the dramatic drop in ages of brides and grooms at initial marriage. Since 1890, the average age of initial marriage has declined three years for men, two years for women. This trend toward early marriage deserves parents' attention. Census Bureau figures indicate clearly that early marriages, especially those involving younger teen-agers, are relatively unsuccessful when compared with other marriages. Often they end rather abruptly in divorce.

Understand the facts about teen-age marriages. The term *teen-age marriage* refers to a union in which both partners or one of them is less than twenty years old. Most teen-age marriages involve a teen-age bride and a groom who is beyond his teens. As a rule, the young man is not in school. He is usually working at a trade and making enough money to support himself and his bride in a modest fashion. The bride is usually a junior or a senior in high school, although she may be less advanced educationally than this or, on the other hand, she may be a high school graduate. If she is in school, chances are four to one she will drop out of school when she gets married, will never return to complete her education.

Boys and girls from low socio-economic status homes marry generally at an earlier age than youngsters from middle- and upper-status homes. This finding reflects the cultural expectations of these groups of parents with reference to their children: middle- and upper-class parents expect their youngsters to postpone marriage until they have finished college; lower-class parents generally expect their sons and daughters to complete high school or less, then go to work, get married, have a family.

Teen-age marriages are usually more risky than marriages by couples in their twenties or thirties. They are stormier, less stable, unhappier; they end more often in separation, annulment or divorce. Marriages in which both partners are less than twenty years old end in divorce twice as often as marriages of partners twenty to twenty-five years old, three times as often as marriages between partners thirty years old. Thus, the chances for success in marriage increase statistically with additional age and maturity of the bride and groom.

Researches reveal that more than half of all teen-age marriages in which both the bride and the groom are still enrolled in high school are forced by pregnancy, a factor believed to be generally harmful to marital adjustment. The least successful teen-age marriages are those that involve a teen-age schoolboy and a teen-age schoolgirl who get married solely because the girl is pregnant. These unions—known as "shot-gun weddings"—are the butt of many jokes. A large percentage of them are dissolved soon after the baby comes. Dr. Judson Landis and Mary Landis found in a study of seventy-five California high schools that such marriages tend to collapse. A similar study in Nebraska by another investigator showed that among 240 married couples of school age, only sixteen couples were still living together after five years.

Forced by pregnancy, too, are perhaps 20 to 30 per cent of all teen-age marriages in which the groom is beyond the teens. In many instances, the couple intended to get married but not so soon. These "hurried-up" marriages are much more successful than "shot-gun" affairs, in which there was no intention to marry until pregnancy made it necessary to choose among criminal abortion, motherhood out of wedlock, or an unwanted wedding to legitimatize the baby. "Hurried-up" marriages end in divorce more often, however, than teen-age marriages in which a year or two passes before a baby comes.

Any teen-ager may be a candidate for early marriage. Research data suggest certain characteristics, however, that are common to youngsters who marry when young. Dr. Lee Burchinal of the University of Iowa found that the girls in his study who married early, in contrast to those who waited, had started dating at a younger-than-average age, had dated more frequently than most girls, had begun going steady earlier, had gone steady more often, had been in love with more boys, had become serious with boys sooner and more often, had mixed with more friends who were married, had more often dated men who were older than themselves, and more often had mothers who had married young.

Joel Moss and Ruby Gingles found in a study of several thousand Nebraska high school students that girls who married young, as compared with those who did not marry young, were emotionally less stable, had less satisfactory relationships with their parents, had more likely begun dating earlier, had had more serious dating relationships (i.e. with sexual involvement), had less frequently planned to attend college, and had less frequently reported that their parents wanted them to go to college, although there were no apparent differences between the two groups in the ability of parents to pay for a college education.

Thus, the characteristic behavior patterns of girls who get married at an early age seem to reflect the parents' economic class or social status, their modest level of aspiration for their youngsters, and, in many instances, their serious neglect of parental responsibilities.

Understand why youth leaders generally oppose teen-age marriages. Responsible leaders of youth are concerned about teen-age marriages because they fail too often. Furthermore, teen-age marriages usually interrupt the partners' education, often terminate it. Many girls and most boys who marry before they are twenty years old are not emotionally mature enough to face realistically the problems of parenthood; yet the most common age for initial pregnancy and motherhood in wedlock today is eighteen years. Vocationally, teen-age boys and many young men who marry teen-age girls are not yet prepared through education, training and experience to make a good living; furthermore, they limit their opportunities for future advancement when forced, by marrying early, to terminate their education.

School administrators vary in their attitudes toward married teen-agers' remaining in school. Some of them would exclude all married students, others would exclude none. Most of them disapprove generally of student marriages but want to do whatever they can to help youngsters who do get married. Here, for example, is a statement by Dr. Glenn Vaniman, a superintendent of schools who represents the more insightful, acceptant point of view: "We don't condone early marriages; however, we recognize them and accept them whenever they occur in our schools. We used to require that students notify us in writing two weeks before the wedding; however, we eliminated that requirement as being impractical. We feel that if students have the permission of their parents, as is required by law, that's enough.

"We encourage students who get married to remain in school if they possibly can. If they don't drop out, we. require that they attend school regularly and maintain good grades; in these respects, they're to be no different from unmarried students. We permit them all the rights and benefits of the regular school program, including athletics and other extracurricular activities. We don't believe, as do some administrators, that married students are a bad influence on those who aren't married.

"If a married girl gets pregnant, she may remain in school as long as she is physically and socially able to do so; we believe in recognizing pregnancy in a married girl as normal, a part of marriage and of life. Unmarried girls who get pregnant, however, aren't allowed in class. If they want to remain registered in our district, we send a teacher to their home an hour each day to give them instruction in private. We do this for the girl's own protection and for the welfare of the community."

A minister who also represents an acceptant point of view says this: "I'm not opposed to young marriages per se; however, the couple should realize they're flirting with real dangers. My wife and I were married just before we were nineteen years old; theoretically, our chances for success weren't good. But here we are today, twenty-four years of happy marriage behind us, four wonderful children, the promise of many more years of joy ahead.

"My wife worked to support us while I went to college and seminary. We postponed our family until I had completed my education.

"Early pregnancies take away freedom, so I feel young couples are wise to postpone their families. Unfortunately, many young couples get married because there's a baby on the way, and this fact puts a strike or two against the marriage before it begins.

"If a young couple builds their home and life around the church, lets it become the hub of social life, the marriage will succeed.

"I have married many hundreds of young couples; only two of them have ended in divorce. Of course, I don't marry everyone who comes to me. I counsel them first in the areas of sexual relations, budget, social adjustment, and spiritual life. If I feel they're definitely not ready for marriage, I advise strongly against it. I tell them I can't marry them until I feel they have a reasonably good chance of success."

Understand the factors that may cause teen-agers to want to get married. Some couples want to get married quickly because, as mentioned earlier, the girl is pregnant. However, there are many other reasons, some of which have been identified through objective research.

Being married implies being grown up. Teen-agers long to be grown up, to be independent, to be free. They want to possess the symbols of adulthood, wear them, display them before they have attained the level of maturity these symbols imply. Thus, teen-agers yearn for marriage in the same way they yearn for cars, for a place of their own, for valuable personal belongings—things that symbolize maturity.

Many teen-agers enjoy the romantic illusion that marriage is a perpetual state of bliss, an eternity of love-making that melts away life's problems. They think miracles will occur when they are married to the "one and only."

Teen-agers tend to be fatalistic about the choice of a marriage partner. Most of them think "the right person" will come along some day, and love will happen— unmistakable, certain love. They will know when they are in love with "the right person" because it will be so wonderful they cannot mistake it. When "the right person" comes along, the two of them will get married; everything will be wonderful. So goes the teen-ager's dream.

Dr. Lee Burchinal in *Sex Ways in Fact and Faith* suggests ten factors that probably influence couples to marry young:

1. Young people look for emotional security in marriage; their anxieties about the times in which we live may cause them to marry earlier than before.

2. Young people look on marriage as a legitimate way to immediate satisfactions, such as love, sex, companionship, parenthood.

3. Recent wars (World War II; the Korean Action) stimulated people to marry young. Continuing threats of war and compulsory military service for older boys tend to

sustain the high rate of youthful marriages.

4. The attitude, *Other kids are getting married; maybe I should get married too,* probably causes some youngsters

to get married.

5. Young people are taught through various commercial

media that marriage is very romantic, an end in itself; therefore, they get married because they think matrimony will melt their problems away.

6. Teen-agers today are more able to make a fairly good living because of prosperous times, working wives, fringe benefits. Furthermore, parents often help young married couples financially.

7. Modern teen-agers get involved earlier in hetero sexual relationships that lead to marriage: early dating, going steady, week-end dating, automobile riding, parking

and petting, sexual intercourse.

8. Movies, magazines, television, books, and other mass media glorify physical love, stimulate young people to act out their sexual urges.

9. Young people who are maladjusted or deficient socially and emotionally may get married trying to resolve their maladjustment or deficiencies.

10. Marriage means "escape" for some young people: escape from home, from parents, from school, from the home town, or from something else they detest.

Many youthful marriages are admittedly based on genuine love, mature judgment, carefully considered plans and honest evaluations by both partners of the chances and the risks. That is why young marriages, in spite of their over-all poor record, succeed generally more often than they fail.

Encourage teen-agers to put off marriage until they are ready to meet the responsibilities of marriage and parenthood. A young couple's chances for success in marriage increase, as a rule, as the couple becomes older. Of course, this does not mean a couple should postpone the wedding until they are old and feeble, hoping thereby to avoid divorce. It does mean, however, that waiting a while—a year or two, perhaps three—rather than plunging headlong into a youthful marriage definitely increases the chances for success. Some youngsters refuse to wait because they are afraid the partner will change his mind and call off the marriage; later, in many cases, they wish they had permitted the partner this privilege, since doing so would have avoided heartbreak, failure, divorce.

There is usually little to lose and much to gain by waiting a while to get married. It is ordinarily advisable, therefore, to encourage teen-agers to take their time, to get fully prepared to accept the responsibilities of marriage and parenthood before they sign the marriage contract.

Understand the requirements for successful marriage; evaluate your teen-ager's qualifications against these standards. Couples who are in love during courtship are more likely to be happy in marriage than those who simply like each other. However, being in love is not in itself enough to make a go of marriage. Being in love is an illusion, however pleasant, that gives way ordinarily to reality, which may or may not be pleasant. Fortunately, the postnuptial reality that partners face who get married while in love is usually acceptable. In some cases, however, when the illusion of being in love disappears, there is nothing left to sustain the marriage; consequently, it disintegrates.

What factors are most often associated with successful marriage? The most important ones are these:

Emotional maturity. Partners are emotionally mature

who face themselves and the world realistically, rationally, calmly. They are not easily upset, hysterical, argumentative or hostile.

Social maturity. Partners are socially mature who enjoy being with others but are not dependent upon them for satisfactions that can come from themselves.

Religious maturity. Partners are religiously mature who know clearly what they believe with reference to the supernatural and have resolved important religious differences that exist between them.

Financial stability. Partners are financially stable who have adequate income to meet their normal needs, who manage their money intelligently, who are not seriously in debt.

Occupational adequacy. Partners are occupational^ adequate when the breadwinner has established himself in an occupation he likes, intends to pursue, and in which he enjoys opportunities for advancement.

Educational adequacy. Partners are educationally adequate when they have completed the highest level of formal schooling necessary to establish occupational adequacy as defined above.

Sexual adequacy. Partners are sexually adequate who are able to have normal sexual relations, enjoy them, gain satisfaction from having them. (This definition does not imply, however, that premarital relations are necessary or desirable.)

Adequate feelings of mutuality. Partners have adequate feelings of mutuality who share their lives willingly, who genuinely enjoy each other socially as well as sexually.

The above list of factors in successful marriage is not exhaustive; it will serve, however, as a helpful checklist for assessing informally your youngster's readiness for marriage.

Many teen-agers get married who are not ready for marriage by the above criteria. They get married generally on short acquaintance, with a very brief engagement period. Being unprepared, they must make a host of adjustments early in marriage that strain the marital relationship: work, school, home, families-in-law. Problems are intensified when there is premarital pregnancy.

Money is often a complicating factor in young marriages. For example, two-thirds of the sixty women Dr. Burchinal interviewed who married when they were still enrolled in high school said they had lived—some time or continuously after the wedding—with in-laws because they had little money. Approximately 40 per cent of them said they had received direct financial assistance from relatives. More than half of them (55 per cent) said they wished they had finished high school before getting married; less than half of them (45 per cent) said they would do the same thing over—get married in high school and drop out. Burchinal believes financial inadequacy is a major cause of maladjustment in youthful marriages, making partners overly dependent on parents and other relatives.

Encourage teen-agers to take courses in school that will help them succeed as marriage partners and as parents. "If young men and women spent as much time preparing for the marriage licenses as they do for their drivers' licenses, our divorce rate would be lowered considerably," said the late Dr. Abraham Stone, physician, author, pioneer leader in education for marriage, parenthood, and related fields. Most people would undoubtedly be more successful in marriage if they would spend some of their thousands of hours of classroom instruction studying courses specifically designed to make them better marriage partners and more effective parents.

Homemaking courses have for many years helped junior and senior high school girls learn such skills as cooking, sewing, household management. These skills are very helpful in marriage; however, they do not get to the fundamental, underlying sources that usually make or break a marriage. Some homemaking teachers know this fact, try to overcome it by teaching marriage relations, baby care, and other important subjects. Margaret Coleman's study of fifty homemaking teachers' instruction showed, however, that homemaking courses are generally devoted almost exclusively to education and training for performing household tasks; they do not prepare young-sters for the all-important psychosocial-sexual aspects of marriage. Coleman found, for example, that only one-fortieth of the time in such classes is spent on family rela-tions; one-sixtieth to child development; practically no time at all to housing or consumer buying; none at all to psychological, social, and sexual problems of marriage partners.

Courses in education for marriage and successful parenthood are being taught in many high schools today, mostly by teachers of social studies who have special training in psychology, sociology, marriage and family living, and related subjects. These courses are designed specifically for the purpose their names imply—to educate and train youngsters to be better marriage partners, more effective parents. The need for meaningful courses such as these is obvious when one considers the high divorce rate among young marriage partners, the high illegitimacy rate, the high abortion rate—to say nothing of the skyrocketing rate of juvenile delinquency and crime that results in part, at least, from parental inadequacies and neglect.

The effectiveness of such courses is summarized by Dr. Evelyn Duvall: "There is evidence from a number of research sources that students who take such courses are more willing to face their problems of sex, courtship, and marriage; more often postpone or break off going steady; are more apt to terminate unpromising engagements; attempt to appraise their love feelings in terms of adequacy for marriage; and postpone marriage until they are prepared to assume the roles and responsibilities that make successful marriages."[2]

Well-intentioned but misinformed critics of the public schools have condemned such courses as being "frills." These people are wrong in almost every instance. Any course that definitely helps youngsters succeed in marriage, avoid divorce, and become conscientious, effective parents is not, by any stretch of the imagination, a "frill." If your youngster's school offers a course in education

[2] Duvall, Evelyn, "Research Finds: Student Marriages," *Marriage and Family Living,* February 1960, p. 77.

for marriage and parenthood, encourage him to take it—and take it seriously. If your school offers none, you will be doing your community a favor when you ask the school administrator and the board of education to install one. The importance to youth of such a course when marriage is so imminent cannot be overestimated.

Dr. Judson Landis, University of California, surveyed the nation recently, found an increasing number of high schools are offering practical courses in marriage and parenthood. He says, however, that America's schools are only beginning to assume their rightful responsibility in this task.

Do everything you can at home to help your teen-ager prepare for marriage and parenthood. Schools can only complement and supplement parental guidance toward successful marriage; they cannot replace it. Conscientious parents develop feelings, attitudes, and values in their children that will make them good marriage partners and effective parents. They instill these basic factors in early life, during the years of infancy and early childhood. They renew them, reinforce them with new experiences, reinterpret them, give them new meanings during the middle years of childhood, preadolescence, and adolescence. Thus, the instillation of feelings, attitudes, and values regarding marriage and parenthood—as well as toward other life tasks—is a continuous process from birth to maturity.

Setting your own good example of happiness in marriage is probably the most effective way you can help your children prepare for successful marriage. "Few factors are more important in predicting marital happiness for youngsters than is happiness in their parents' marriage," says Dr. Mary Jane Hungerford of the American Institute of Family Relations. Researches reveal that children of happily married parents make better marriage partners, get divorces less frequently, become better parents than do unhappily married parents' children, many of whom separate or divorce. Youngsters tend to emulate their parents. If the parents' marriage is really worth emulating, it helps the youngster develop a wholesome image of marital success that he may, in time, fulfill in his own life.

Teaching a daughter the fundamentals of homemaking and home management enhances her chances for success in these aspects of marriage. Being a housewife is a difficult job, an important one that deserves to be done well. The modern teen-age girl should know how to operate all household equipment and appliances a house-wife uses ordinarily; how to plan menus, cook, bake, manage kitchen and meals; how to select and purchase intelligently all furnishings for the home; how to sew, knit, mend; how to organize housework, accomplish it efficiently; and many other skills. These are the kinds of things girls a few generations ago were expected to know —indeed, to have mastered—before they got married. It is not uncommon to meet brides today who are so ignorant about such things they say innocently to the groom: "I do hope you'll show me how to fry an egg. That's the only way I'll ever be able to fix our breakfast." All too often, they are not kidding; they are serious.

Girls should have experience in baby and child care before they marry. Boys probably should too, for that matter. Girls who have taken care of younger siblings have a distinct advantage as a rule when they themselves become mothers. They know what to do with a baby, when and how to do it. Girls who have had baby sitting experience also go into marriage with a clearer picture of what they are likely to encounter some day. Unfortunately, many parents protect their daughters too much for their own good, deny them the privilege of learning about babies and small children, do not permit them to earn money of their own. They give them too much allowance, too many material goods. They indulge them too much, expect too little of them in return. They would do them a favor if they encouraged them to learn more about the realities of family living.

Boys and girls alike should know the value of a dollar before they marry. Perhaps the best way they can learn this lesson is to supplement their allowance with money they earn outside the home. They should be permitted to manage it themselves with a minimum of supervision by parents.

Parents may help too by praising their youngsters for the kinds of behavior that may make them better marriage partners, more effective parents: honesty, integrity, helpfulness, objectivity, economy, neat grooming, good housekeeping, superior cooking and baking, intelligent money management, and many other qualities and abilities.

Parents' attitudes toward sex are usually quite apparent to children, even the younger ones. Teen-agers, however, become especially aware of the feelings of sexuality that exist—or do not exist—between their parents. Parents' attitudes reveal themselves in a variety of ways, most of them quite subtle. Teen-agers feel reassured that marriage *is* worthwhile when they sense that their parents are good companions sexually as well as in other ways.

Parents are wise who take a wholesome attitude toward sex in their own lives and in the lives of their children. They accept sex as fact and sexual feelings as normal, desirable aspects of human life. They teach their children the purposes and meanings of sex in terms they can understand. They help their youngsters identify themselves correctly and adequately as members of their own sex, avoid the confusion in sex roles that inevitably would invite disaster into their adult lives. They continue reinforcing these feelings and attitudes through middle childhood, preadolescence, and adolescence. Thus, their sons, when old enough to marry, know that they are definitely masculine; they are ready and eager to play adequately the role of husband and father. Likewise, their daughters, when ready to marry, know that they are definitely feminine; they are ready and willing to fulfill their role as wife and mother. These are the kinds of youngsters who become good husbands and wives, effective parents, genuine assets to the community.

Parents may help their teen-agers prepare sexually for marriage by listening patiently to their problems, understanding how they feel, discussing their concerns with them, answering their questions when they (the parents) know the answers, securing authoritative books for teen-agers to read when the parents do not know the answers.

Recognize in your youngsters' boyfriends and girlfriends the factors that might suggest they are good prospects for marriage. Parents should observe much and say little about their adolescents' friends. Teen-agers, being independence-seekers, usually resent parents' comments about their friends, especially the negative criticisms they feel are undeserved. Parents are wise who look carefully and listen intelligently.

Research findings, which provide important clues, suggest that young couples are more likely to make a go of marriage who, prior to marriage, get along well together, seldom quarrel, enjoy similar interests, become thoroughly acquainted, are genuinely themselves when they are together, enjoy each other's friends, are fond of their own parents, are fond of each other's parents, have the same religious convictions, are sensible about money, share similar attitudes, share the same values, are affectionate toward each other, have respect for each other, and postpone sexual relations until after the wedding.

It would be foolhardy, perhaps wrong, to try to influence your youngster to marry someone merely because the two of them seem "made for each other" or to influence him in the other direction if the candidate seems wrong for him. A levelheaded, intelligent young person will usually make the correct decision on his own if permitted to do so, and will profit from the decision-making experience. Yet parents must be considered negligent who stand by passively and permit their youngster to marry someone whom they think is a bad prospect for marriage. They should at least let their youngster know how they feel; perhaps their attitudes will cause him to postpone the marriage or to reconsider—which, in itself, may increase the possibilities for successful marriage.

If your teen-ager is considering marriage, encourage him to get premarital counseling from a qualified marriage counselor. Researches suggest strongly that young people who are considering marriage should have premarital counseling. Husbands and wives who had counseling prior to marriage are overwhelmingly more successful in marriage than couples who had no premarital counseling. This fact does not necessarily mean, of course, that premarital counseling itself caused couples to succeed in marriage; perhaps they would have been as happy in marriage without premarital counseling as they are having had it—there is no way of knowing. Nevertheless, young couples who get counseling, advice, education, and training for marriage and parenthood do actually perform much better in marriage than those who do not have such experiences. This fact suggests that these youngsters want to learn, are willing to think as well as feel about the problems and responsibilities of marriage before they say, "I do."

If your teen-ager is going to get married, encourage him to have a thorough premarital medical examination. Most states require a premarital medical examination of the prospective bride and groom, mainly to determine the presence or absence of venereal disease. A thorough premarital examination, however, goes much further.

A minimal examination of the prospective bride, according to Nadina R. Kavinoky, M.D., a prominent gynecologist and former President of the National Council on Family Relations, includes a complete medical history, thorough pelvic examination, detection of any abnormalities, defects, or deficiencies, and correction of them if possible, explanation of the physiology and psychology of marital relations, explanation of family planning and birth control, fitting of a contraceptive device if one is desired, explanation of the rhythm cycle to brides who prefer it. The bride returns to the gynecologist after the honeymoon for a check-up and re-evaluation.

Prospective grooms should be given equally thorough examination and information by the physician, preferably a urologist who is interested professionally in the marital success of his patients. If the young man doubts his own ability to become a father (a common fear among first-time grooms), a simple laboratory test may either reassure him that he is normally fertile or suggest that he initiate medical treatment to increase his degree of fertility until it is normal.

It is obviously better that young men and young women know the medical facts about themselves before they get married rather than remain ignorant, perhaps worrying needlessly that they are not normal. Review of major points

1. Understand the facts about marital failure and divorce in modern America.
2. Understand the facts about teen-age marriages.
3. Understand why youth leaders generally oppose teen-age marriages.
4. Understand the factors that may cause teen-agers to want to get married.
5. Encourage your teen-agers to wait for marriage until they are really ready to meet the responsibilities of marriage and parenthood.
6. Understand the requirements for successful marriage; evaluate your teen-ager's qualifications against these standards.
7. Encourage your teen-agers to take courses in school that will help them succeed as marriage partners and as parents.
8. Do everything you can at home to help your teen ager prepare for marriage and parenthood.
9. Recognize in your youngsters' boyfriends and girl friends the factors that might suggest they are good prospects for marriage.

10. If your teen-ager is considering marriage, encourage him to get premarital counseling from a qualified marriage counselor.
11. If your teen-ager is going to get married, encourage him to get a thorough premarital medical examination.

SUMMARY

This chapter discussed marriage and parenthood and suggested ways parents can help their teen-ager prepare for successful marriage and effective parenthood.

This chapter concludes the text of this book. There follow a brief conclusion and a list of selected books, films, and pamphlet sources for parents and teen-agers.

Conclusion

The adolescent years, which provide the link between childhood and maturity, are often the most dramatic ones in life. Youngsters move gradually away from their parents during this period and assert themselves with increasing vigor—a normal development that causes many tensions and stresses in the home, at school, and in the community.

Teen-agers need parents today more than they have ever needed them before. They need parents who encourage them to face life's problems realistically, courageously, persistently, not as children nor as adults, but as adolescents.

You, the thoughtful, conscientious parent, want sincerely to help your teen-ager grow up and become eventually a creative, responsible adult. There are many things you can do to accomplish this goal, among which are these:

1. Recognize and appreciate the problems your teenager faces.

2. Understand normal adolescent growth and development, especially as it relates to your teen-ager.

3. Understand how your teen-ager feels about himself, and give him whatever emotional support he needs.

4. Encourage your teen-ager to establish and maintain wholesome friendships.

5. Help your teen-ager become socially competent through peer-group relationships.

6. Help your youngster solve his dating problems.

7. Recognize your parental responsibilities for supervising or controlling certain dating practices.

8. Help your teen-ager develop wholesome attitudes about sex.

9. Face the problem of teen-agers and automobiles realistically and constructively.

10. Help your youngster get the most out of junior high and high school.

11. Help your teen-ager learn about work and money.

12. Help your youngster prepare for college if he is mentally able to profit from it.

13. Help your teen-ager reinforce sound moral and spiritual values.

14. Teach your youngster to accept the responsibilities of citizenship in a democratic society.

15. Help your teen-ager prepare for the responsibilities of marriage and parenthood.

Selected Books, Films, and Pamphlet Sources

Books, pamphlets, and films about adolescents are often useful to parents in helping teen-agers grow up. The materials listed below may be used by parents in study groups as well as individually. Books indicated by an asterisk (*) are directed to adolescents; they may also be profitably read by adults.

Pamphlets useful to parents are too numerous to list; however, you may request titles from the organizations listed in this section.

Books

1. Bandura, Albert, and Walters, Richard H., *Adolescent Aggression.* New York: Ronald Press Company, 1959.

*2. Beck, Lester F., *Human Growth.* New York: Harcourt, Brace and Company, 1949.

*3. Bockner, Ruth, *Growing Your Own Way.* New York: Abelard-Schuman, Limited, 1959.

*4. Bossard, James H. S., and Boll, Eleanor Stokes, *The Girl That You Marry.* Philadelphia: Macrae Smith Company, 1961.

5. Cleaver, Nancy, *The Treasury of Family Fun.* Westwood, New Jersey: Fleming H. Revell Company, 1960.

*6. Davis, Maxine, *Sex and the Adolescent.* New York: Dial Press, 1958. (Issued paperbound by Permabooks, 1959.)

*7. Duvall, Evelyn M., *Facts of Life and Love for Teen-Agers.* New York: Association Press, 1956. (Issued paper-bound by Popular Library, 1956.)

8. Duvall, Evelyn and Sylvanus, editors, *Sex Ways—In Fact and Faith.* New York: Association Press, 1961.

*9. Duvall, Evelyn M., and Hill, Reuben, *Being Married.* New York: Association Press, 1960.

*10. Duvall, Evelyn M., and Johnson, Joy Duvall, *The Art of Dating.* New York: Association Press, 1958. (Issued paper-bound by Permabooks, 1960.)

*11. Duvall, Sylvanus M., *Before You Marry.* New York: Association Press, 1959.

12. Eckert, Ralph G., *Sex Attitudes in the Home.* New York: Association Press, 1956. (Issued paperbound by Popular Library, 1958.)

13. Ehrmann, Winston, *Premarital Dating Behavior.* New York: Henry Holt Company, 1959. (Issued paperbound by Bantam Books, 1960.)

14. Fairchild, Roy W., and Wynn, John Charles, *Families in the Church: A Protestant Survey.* New York: Association Press, 1961.

15. Farnham, Marynia F·, *The Adolescent.* New York: Harper and Brothers, 1951.

*I6. Fedder, Ruth, *You, The Person You Want to Be.* New York: Whittlesey House, 1957.

*17. Fine, Benjamin, *How to Be Accepted by the College of Your Choice.* New York: Channel Press, Inc., (revised), 1960.

18. Fine, Benjamin, *1,000,000 Delinquents.* New York: The World Publishing Company, 1955.

19. Frank, Mary and Lawrence K., *Your Adolescent at Home and in School.* New York: Viking Press, 1956. (Issued paperbound by New American Library, 1959.)

20. Friedenberg, Edgar Z., *The Vanishing Adolescent.* Boston: Beacon Press, 1959.

21. Gallagher, J. Roswell, *Understanding Your Son's Adolescence.* New York: Little, Brown and Company, 1951.

22. Gallagher, J. Roswell, M.D., and Harris, Herbert I., M.D., *Emotional Problems of Adolescents.* New York: Oxford University Press, 1958.

23. Gesell, Arnold, M.D., Ilg, Frances L., M.D., and Ames, Louise Bates, *Youth: The Years from Ten to Sixteen* New York: Harper Brothers, Inc., 1956.

24. Havighurst, Robert H., and Taba, Hilda, *Adolescent Character and Personality.* New York: John Wiley Sons, 1954.

25. Jersild, Arthur T., *The Psychology of Adolescence.* New York: The Macmillan Company, 1957.

26. Johnson, Eric W., *How to Live Through Junior High School.* Philadelphia: J. B. Lippincott Company, 1959.

27. Kirkendall, Lester A., *Premarital Intercourse and Interpersonal Relationships.* New York: The Julian Press, 1961.

28. Kvaraceus, William, and Miller, Walter, and others, *Delinquent Behavior.* Two volumes. Washington, D.C: National Education Association, 1959.

*29. Landis, Judson and Mary, *Building Your Life.* Engle-wood Cliffs, New Jersey: Prentice-Hall, Inc., 1959.

*30. Landis, Judson and Mary, *Personal Adjustment, Marriage and Family Living.* Englewood Cliffs, New Jersey: Prentice-Hall Inc., 1960.

31. Malm, Marguerite, and Jamison, Olis G., *Adolescence.* New York: McGraw-Hill Book Company, Inc., 1952.

*32. Narramore, Clyde M., *Life and Love.* Grand Rapids, Michigan: Zondervan Publishing House, 1955.

33. Reiss, Ira L., *Premarital Sex Standards in America.* Glencoe, Illinois: The Free Press, 1960.

34. Remmers, H. H., and Radler, D. H., *The American Teen-Ager.* Indianapolis: The Bobbs-Merrill Company, Inc., 1957.

35. Strang, Ruth, *The Adolescent Views Himself.* New York: McGraw-Hill Book Company, 1957.

36. Vincent, Clark E., *Unwed Mothers.* Glencoe, Illinois: The Free Press, 1961.

37. Wittenberg, Rudolph, *On Call for Youth.* New York: Association Press, 1955.

38. Young, Leontine R., *Out of Wedlock.* New York: McGraw-Hill Book Company, Inc., 1954.

Films (16mm sound)

1. *Age of Turmoil.* 20 minutes. (Thirteen-, fourteen-, and fifteen-year-olds giggle, criticize school, behave immaturely in many ways.) Distributed by McGraw-Hill Book Company.

2. *Are You Ready for Marriage?* 15 minutes. (Marriage counselor poses criteria for marriage readiness.) Distributed by Coronet Films.

3. *Choosing for Happiness.* 14 minutes. (Analysis of one's own personality needs is main key to mate selection.) Distributed by McGraw-Hill Book Company.

4. *Discipline During Adolescence.* 16 minutes. (Contrasts effects of various kinds of discipline and punishment of behavior.) Distributed by McGraw-Hill Book Company.

5. *Emotional Maturity.* 20 minutes. (Parents can help teen-agers develop increased emotional maturity.) Distributed by McGraw-Hill Book Company.

6. *Farewell to Childhood.* 23 minutes. (Teen-age girl wants adult independence and privileges but fears the responsibilities. Parents try to understand her inconsistencies.) Distributed by International Film Bureau.

7. *Head of the House.* 37 minutes. (Young adolescent gets into trouble, is befriended by social worker, policeman, minister, parents.) Distributed by United World Films.

8. *The High Wall.* 32 minutes. (Deals with problem of aggressive bigotry, teen-age gang war violence, psychiatric

analysis of motives.) Distributed by McGraw-Hill Book Company.

9. *How Much Affection?* 20 minutes. (High school students try to reconcile their affectional behavior toward one another and their feelings about right and wrong.) Distributed by McGraw-Hill Book Company.

10. *Howard.* 29 minutes. (Older teen-ager develops inner conflict between his desire to follow his own impulses and his need to conform to parents' wishes.) Distributed by International Film Bureau.

11. Is *This Love?* 14 minutes. (How do teen-agers know how to recognize love? Contrasts romances of two girls. Raises questions for discussion.) Distributed by McGraw-Hill Book Company.

12. *It Takes All Kinds.* 20 minutes. (Selection of mate. Careful, intelligent choice of marital partner helps assure success in marriage.) Distributed by McGraw-Hill Book Company.

13. *Marriage is a Partnership.* 16 minutes. (Early years of marriage require couples to face problems of communication, responsibility, decisions, loyalties.) Distributed by Coronet Films.

14. *Meaning of Adolescence.* 16 minutes. (Contrasts teenagers in primitive and modern cultures; overview of social, emotional, mental, physical changes during adolescence.) Distributed by McGraw-Hill Book Company.

15. *Meeting the Needs of Adolescents.* 19 minutes. (A family meets basic physical needs, stimulates mental development, guides spiritual growth of adolescents.) Distributed by McGraw-Hill Book Company.

16. *Parents Are People Too.* 15 minutes. (Parent-adolescent relationship should be one of mutual understanding with room for growth.) Distributed by McGraw-Hill Book Company.

17. *Physical Aspects of Puberty.* 19 minutes. (Physiological aspects of attaining sexual maturity; social behavior and adjustment problems that may accompany puberty.) Distributed by McGraw-Hill Book Company.

18. *Sibling Rivalries and Parents.* 11 minutes. (Siblings grow up in same home and family but have different experiences and reactions; parents may help them adjust.) Distributed by McGraw-Hill Book Company.

19. *Social Acceptability.* 20 minutes. (Teen-ager needs parental guidance and encouragement to develop social skills.) Distributed by McGraw-Hill Book Company.

20. *Social-Sex Attitudes in Adolescence.* 22 minutes. (Parents play key role in developing social competencies and sound judgment regarding sex in teen-agers.) Distributed by McGraw-Hill Book Company.

21. *Story of Menstruation.* 10 minutes. (Walt Disney Studios production shows menstruation as phase of normal female growth and development. Used most often with preadolescents; useful to teen-agers too.) Distributed by International Cellucotton Products Company.

22. *The Teens.* 26 minutes. (Parents try to understand the habits and behavior of adolescents as individuals and in groups.) Distributed by McGraw-Hill Book Company.

23. *This Charming Couple.* 19 minutes. (Teen-age girl falls in love with young instructor; analysis of their personality patterns suggests probable failure if they marry.) Distributed by McGraw-Hill Book Company.

24. *Three Steps to Start.* 26 minutes. (Citizens of community attempt to cope intelligently and constructively with the problem of youth.) Distributed by McGraw-Hill Book Company.

25. *Understanding Ourselves: Human Growth.* 19 minutes. (Facts about human growth and development: physical changes, development, menstruation, fertilization, pregnancy, birth. Widely used with preadolescents; useful to teen-agers too.) Distributed by E. C. Brown Trust.

26. *When Should I Marry?* 19 minutes. (Teen-age boy and girl, eager to marry, talk with minister about problems of early marriage.) Distributed by McGraw-Hill Book Company.

27. *Who Is Sylvia?* 29 minutes. (Fourteen-year-old girl, in period of transition from childhood to womanhood, manifests hopes, dreams, fears; social relationships and the gang.) Distributed by International Film Bureau.

28. *Your Body During Adolescence.* 10 minutes. (Seven glands regulate growth and development during adolescence, cause physical and emotional changes.) Distributed by McGraw-Hill Book Company.

The films listed above may be secured through most film libraries or directly from the distributors, whose office addresses are as follows:

Coronet Films
Coronet Building
Chicago 1, Illinois

E. C. Brown Trust
Education Center Building
220 South West Alder Street
Portland 4, Oregon

International Cellucotton Products Co,
919 North Michigan Avenue
Chicago 11, Illinois

International Film Bureau, Inc·
332 South Michigan Avenue
Chicago 4, Illinois

McGraw-Hill Book Company
Text-Film Department
330 West 42nd Street
New York 18, New York

Educational Film Department
United World Films, Inc.
1445 Park Avenue
New York 29, New York

Television Series

Paging Parents, a public service television series for parents on problems in child-rearing during infancy, childhood, and adolescence. Videotapes and 16mm kinescopes. Twenty-nine minutes each.

Produced by the California Congress of Parents and Teachers, Inc., in cooperation with the Office of the Los Angeles County Superintendent of Schools.

Distributed by the California Congress of Parents and Teachers, Inc., 930 Georgia Street, Los Angeles 15, California.

Sources of Pamphlets and Booklets

The following organizations provide inexpensive pamphlets and booklets that deal with adolescence and other subjects. They will send you a price list of titles on request.

American Dental Association
Division of Dental Health Education
222 East Superior Street
Chicago 11, Illinois

American Institute of Family Relations
5287 Sunset Boulevard
Los Angeles 27, California

American Medical Association
Order Department
535 North Dearborn Street
Chicago 10, Illinois

American Personnel and Guidance Association
1605 New Hampshire Avenue,
N. W. Washington 9, D. C.

American Social Hygiene Association
1790 Broadway
New York 19, New York
Children's Bureau

United States Department of Health, Education
    and Welfare
Washington 25, D. C.

Child Study Association of America
Publications Department
9 East 89th Street
New York 28, New York

Connecticut Mutual Life Insurance Company
Hartford 15
Connecticut

John Hancock Mutual Life Insurance Company
Health Education Service
200 Berkeley Street
Boston 17, Massachusetts

The Hogg Foundation for Mental Health
Mailing Division
The University of Texas
Austin 12, Texas

Metropolitan Life Insurance Company
Health and Welfare Division
1 Madison Avenue
New York 10, New York

National Association for Mental Health
10 Columbus Circle
New York 19, New York

National Education Association
1201 Sixteenth Street, N. W.
Washington 6, D. C.

National Safety Council
425 North Michigan Avenue
Chicago 11, Illinois

Public Affairs Committee
22 East 38th Street
New York 16, New York

Science Research Associates
57 West Grand Avenue
Chicago 10, Illinois

United States Government Printing Office
Superintendent of Documents
Washington 25, D. C.

Index

Also available from www.sunvillagepublications.com

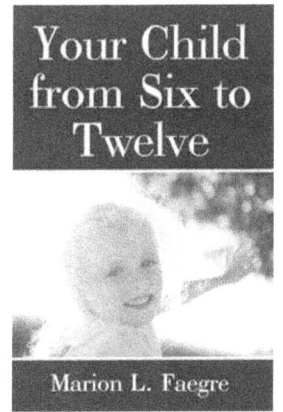

Your Child
from Six to
Twelve

Marion L. Faegre

CHILD TRAINING

A GUIDE TO SUCCESSFUL PARENTHOOD

GLADYS GARDNER JENKINS, M.A.
EDWARD H. STOLKEN, M.A. PH.D.
MARTHA BENNETT KING, B.S.
HARRY ORRIN GILLET, R.S.

The Intelligent
Parents' Guide To
Raising Children

Eve Jones, Ph.D.

87 Ways To
Help Your
Children In
School

William H. Armstrong

How To Help Your
Teenager Grow Up

A Guide To Creative Parenthood
By Leland E. Glover, Ph.D.

How To Help
Your Child
Read Better

Ruth Strang

How To Teach Children
The Joy of Reading

A Guide for Parents and Teachers

Ellen C. Henderson

Launching
Your
Preschooler
How To Help Make Your Child's
First Experiences A Breeze!

Edgar S. Bley

HOW TO PREVENT
STUTTERING IN
CHILDREN
A Guide for Parents and Teachers

Leon Lassers, Ph.D.

Teach Your
Child To Talk

How To Tell
Children
About Sex

Clyde M. Narramore, Ed.D.